The Shield

Russia and the Jewish Question

Russian Intellectuals on anti-Semitism

Published by Alexander Vassiliev

Originally published by Alfred A. Knopf in 1917

Edited by
Maxim Gorky, Leonid Andreyev, and
Fyodor Sologub

Translated from Russian by
A. Yarmolinsky

With a Foreword by
William English Walling

Cover photograph: Jewish water carrier standing in
a street in Vilna, Russia (1922)
Frank Carpenter Collection. Library of Congress
Prints and Photographs Division
Washington, D.C. 20540 USA

Contents

William English Walling, Foreword   5

Preface   15

Maxim Gorky, Russia and the Jews   17

Leonid Andreyev, The First Step   27

Vladimir Korolenko, Mr. Jackson's Opinion on the Jewish Question   39

Paul Milyukov, The Jewish Question in Russia   51

Mikhail Bernatzky, The Jews and Russian Economic Life   65

Prince Paul Dolgorukov, The War and the Status of the Jew   75

Maxim Kovalevsky, Jewish Rights and their Enemies   79

Dmitry Merezhkovsky, The Jewish Question as a Russian Question   87

Vyacheslav Ivanov, Concerning the Ideology of the Jewish Question   93

Maxim Gorky, The Little Boy   97

Fyodor Sologub, The Fatherland for All   103

Vladimir Solovyov, On Nationalism   109

Count Ivan Tolstoy, Concerning the Legal Status of the Jews   111

Leonid Andreyev, The Wounded Soldier   115

Catherine Kuskova, How to Help?   119

Sergey Yelpatyevsky, The Homeless Ones   125

Mikhail Artzibashef, The Jew   133

Foreword

This is not merely a book about the Russian Jews. It is a marvellous revelation of the Russian soul. It shows not only that the overwhelming majority of the Russian intellectuals, including nearly all of her brilliant literary geniuses, are opposed to the persecution of the Jews or any other race, but that they have a capacity for sympathy and understanding of humanity unequalled in any other land. I do not know of any book where the genius and heart of Russia is better displayed. Not only her leading litterateurs but also her leading statesmen and economists are represented—and all of them speak as with a single voice.

I am writing on the 16th of March. Yesterday the news reached the world that Russia had probably at last succeeded in emancipating itself from the German-sustained and German-supported autocracy which so long has been renounced by practically all classes of the Russian people. I have pointed out elsewhere that this Second Act of the great drama of social transformation in Russia was to be expected in connection with the present war. It is not surprising that this Act, like the first—the Revolution of 1905—is accompanied by an irresistible demand for the cessation of the persecution of the Jews and other minority races. The first Duma, that of 1906, demanded unanimously that all these races be given absolutely the same rights as other Russians. The rise of Liberalism during the war, in connection with military necessities, had already

5

abolished a number of Jewish disabilities. There is no longer any question that the Jews will be given equality. Without exception the anti-Semitic organisations were supported by the pro-German party, the money which was alone responsible for the pogroms was furnished by these same organisations, and now this Party and these organisations are forever overthrown. It was Dr. Dubrovin, for example, who year by year carried out the murders of the leading representatives of the Jews in the Duma and who almost succeeded in having Milyukov assassinated a few weeks ago. Dubrovin was one of the most important of the sinister forces supported by the money of the German Czarina's court party—which was organised by Baron Fredericks and other notorious Germans masquerading as Russians.

The re-birth of Russia which is now taking place cannot be understood apart from the Jewish problem. As Russia's leading Liberal statesman, Prof. Paul Milyukov—who is well and favorably known in America because of extended visits here—points out in the article he contributes to the present volume, the anti-Semitic parties coincide with the anti-constitutional parties. At first this seems a strange and unaccountable fact, but a brief glance at the history of other countries will show that the party standing for the persecution of weak foreign neighbours and the oppression of minority races within and without a country has always and everywhere been the party of reaction. As Milyukov says, there was no need for an anti-constitutional movement until there was a constitutional movement. As soon as Liberalism appeared, however, and gained support among the masses, it was necessary to fabricate some counter movement, and the governmental bureaucracy fixed upon anti-Semitism as a primitive means of appealing to the masses, and so of bridling them. It may be further pointed out that this systematic propaganda against democracy was almost non-existent in Russia until it had become thoroughly organised and successful in Germany. Both Kovalevsky and Milyukov demonstrate in the present volume that anti-Semitism became an important factor in Russian life only after the middle of the Nineteenth Century—that is to say, after the final victory of Prussian Reactionism over German Liberalism in 1849 (a victory which has lasted to the present time)—and still more, after the great military victories of Prussia from 1864 to 1870 had put Prussian militarism in the saddle and had made it the dominating force in the Russian court and Russian bureaucracy.

However, the intelligence, energy, and courage of the Russian Liberals has entirely thwarted this scheme to divide the Russian people. The bureaucracy has gained almost no support among any section of the Russian nation, except its own narrow circles, either for its persecution of the Jews or its oppression of the Poles, Finns, Tartars, Armenians and other races. On the contrary, the anti-Semitic propaganda has reacted against its promoters. A considerable number, though by no means a majority, of the Russian Liberals are Jews, and Russian Liberals do not at all endeavour to hide this fact. The consequence is that the union of the Russian Liberals with all the persecuted races has been all the more firmly cemented. And just as all Russian Liberals are ardent supporters of the war against Germany, so practically all the leaders of the Russian Jews are equally patriotic—in spite of the fact that many forms of persecution have remained, and, furthermore, new forms of persecution have been invented since the war. Though the German agitation in America has won over a large part of the Russian Jews in this country to the German cause, this agitation has had no such success in Russia, unless among a relatively small proportion of the Jewish population.

It is known that the anti-Semitic agitation in Russia has taken hold of only a small proportion of the Russian people among the semi-criminal population of the cities and towns. It is notorious that the pogroms were often organised and carried out by the secret police and the cossacks, and that in other instances they were executed by bands of a few hundred bribed toughs, called by educated Russians "the black hundreds." This social element is what we would ordinarily call in America the "mob," and it certainly does not constitute one per cent of the population in Russia or in any other country. Gorky refers to it as "the populace": "In addition to the people, there is also the 'populace,' something standing outside of social classes and outside of civilisation, and united by the dark sense of hatred against all that surpasses its understanding and is defenceless against brute force. I speak of the populace which thus defines itself in the words of Pushkin:

"We are insidious and shameless,
Ungrateful, faint-hearted and wicked;
At heart we are cold, sterile eunuchs,
Traducers, born to slavery.'"

The refusal of the Russian people to be either bribed or deceived into hostility to the Jews is clearly enough demonstrated by the feeling of affection on the part of most intelligent Jews towards the Russian people. The

8

only exceptions are those Jews which come from the Polish cities far within the Jewish Pale and do not know the Russian people except by hearsay. Unfortunately, this is a considerable portion of the total of the Jews in Russia, and it is from these cities and towns in the heart of the Pale that most of our immigrants come. But all the more educated Jews—and a very large part are educated—all those who know Russia either by a travel or through Russian literature and newspapers, feel a deep affection for their country, for in spite of all, Russia belongs to them just as much as it does to other Russians. One of the editors of the present volume, Fyodor Sologub, says: "Whenever I met Russian Jews abroad, I always marvelled at the strangely tenacious love for Russia which they preserve. They speak of Russia with the same longing and the same tenderness as the Russian emigrants; they are equally eager to return and equally saddened, if the return is impossible. Wherefore should they love Russia, who is so harsh and inhospitable toward them?"

It is useless for Americans to deceive themselves into thinking that the Russian Jewish question is either unimportant or incomprehensible from the point of view of our progress and democracy. Do we not have our negro and Asiatic problems? Do not the English have their Irish and Indian questions? I do not suggest that the parallel is complete, but it is clear that the Russian writers in the present volume are perfectly correct in referring both to our negro question and our question of yellow labour as closely similar to their Jewish problem. Both the brilliant and fascinating discussions by Andreyev and Merezhkovsky will apply almost as well to any other so-called "race question" as to that of the Russian Jews. Says Merezhkovsky: "We would like very much to say that there is no such thing as the Jewish, Polish, Ukrainian, Armenian, Georgian, question; that there is only one question—the Russian. Yes, we would like to, but we cannot; the Russian people have yet to earn the right to say that, and therein lies their tragedy...."

"'Judophilism' and 'Judophobia' are closely related. A blind denial of a nationality engenders an equally blind affirmation of it. An absolute 'Nay' naturally brings forth an absolute 'Yea.'"

"That is why we say to the 'Nationalists': 'Cease oppressing the non-Russian element of our empire, so that we may have the right to be Russians, and that we may with dignity show our national face, as that of a human being, not that of a beast. Cease to be 'Judophobes' so that we may cease to be 'Judophiles.'"

Is it not clear from the recent discussion in the British Parliament that the Irish problem weighs like an almost intolerable burden just as much upon the British Empire as it does upon Ireland? Is it not equally clear from England's concession of a cotton tariff to India that she will be obliged for her own sake to make further concessions to justice in that country? And can America ever hope to have any standing in the court of nations as long as our infamous persecution of the negroes and our atrocious attitude towards Asiatics continues? Nations can indulge themselves for a certain period in such gross and stupid crimes, but the longer the settlement is postponed the greater the blood-price that must be paid in the end—and in the meanwhile all our civilisation is poisoned, if not actually rotted, by the network of lies by which the persecutors are forced to defend their infamies—lies which are necessarily more far-reaching and impudently false in a democracy than they are in an autocracy where the existing system maintains itself rather by force than by public opinion.

But few of us educated Americans have the intellectual and moral courage of the educated classes of Russia. We feel that we can avoid our moral and intellectual responsibilities by turning our back on existing crimes. It has frequently been pointed out that in spite of a government even more anti-democratic than that of Germany, the Russian people have been infinitely more democratic than the Germans. In the same way, while the institutions of America are much further developed in the direction of general democracy than those of Russia, the very reverse is the case with public opinion. The educated classes of Russia have the courage and intelligence to call a spade a spade. They realise that they are partly responsible for the sins committed by the Russian nation, even though they have been powerless heretofore to remedy these conditions in the face of an armed and organised autocracy, backed by the moral, intellectual and military force of Germany and by the money of France and England. Andreyev, for example, regards the Jewish problem as primarily a Russian problem. It is one of the chief burdens, if not the chief burden, which has been crushing the Russian nation. In this book he says: "When did the 'Jewish question' leap on my back?—I do not know. I was born with it and under it. From the very moment I assumed a conscious attitude towards life until this very day I have lived in its noisome atmosphere, breathed in the poisoned air which surrounds all these 'problems,' all these dark, harrowing alogisms, unbearable to the intellect... And yet I, a Russian intellectual, a happy representative of the sovereign race, although fully conscious and convinced that the 'Jewish question' is no question at all,—I felt powerless and doomed to the most sterile tribulation of spirit. For, all the clear-cut arguments of my intellect, the most fervent tirades and speeches, the sincerest tears of compassion and outcries of indignation unfailingly broke against a dull, unresponsive wall. But all powerlessness, if it is unable to prevent a crime, becomes complicity; and this was the result: personally guiltless of any offence against my brother, I have become in the eyes of all those unconcerned and those of my brother himself, a Cain."

The new Russia is being born while I write these lines, and intelligent Americans are discussing nothing else except this great world event—comparable in importance even to the colossal war itself. If we wish to understand educated Russia—which has brought about the change—many-sided, large-hearted and intellectually more brilliant perhaps than the educated class of any other nation, we cannot do better than to read and think over what that galaxy of Russian genius that has composed the present volume has written. We must not forget that the educated class in Russia is almost as numerous as in the other great nations, and perhaps plays an even more important role in Russia than it does in other countries. What Russia has lacked has been neither an educated class nor masses capable and ready to be trained to any kind of modern employment, but a great technically trained, free and organised "intellectual middle class"—an expression I am forced to coin for my present purpose. It is hardly necessary to prove this assertion. The world is well acquainted with

Russian genius in literature, art, music, philosophy, sociology, economics, history, and the higher realms of science. Moreover Russia is not without technological schools, but the proportion of her population employed in the scientific organisation of industry and business is insignificant in comparison with that of other countries—owing, of course, to the backward state of Russian industry and Russian government. But this fact, important as it is, must not obscure the equally important fact that the educated and cultivated class in Russia, speaking several languages, and personally familiar with the civilisation of one or more foreign countries, exercises an influence over Russian society and Russian public opinion undoubtedly stronger than that of any other educated class whatever—with the possible exception of that of Germany. We cannot hope to understand the new Russia unless we understand the character and point of view of the Russian "intelligentsia," and this is nowhere so clearly, succinctly and interestingly set forth as in "The Shield."

William English Walling
Greenwich, Connecticut

By William Allen Rogers, 1854-1931.
Library of Congress Prints and Photographs Division
Washington, D.C. 20540 USA

Preface

Published by the Russian Society for the Study of Jewish Life under the joint editorship of three eminent men-of-letters, Gorky, Andreyev, and Sologub, the original Shield saw the light of day last year in Petrograd. The book consists of numerous studies, essays, stories and poems, all these contributions to the symposium on the Jewish question coming exclusively from the pen of Russian authors of non-Jewish birth. In making a selection for the present volume, I have thought it advisable to give decided preference to the publicistic articles of the original collection. Thus, the present version contains practically all the various important studies and essays of the Russian Shield, while most of the stories have been omitted, without great detriment to the book. I have also had to sacrifice, for obvious reasons, all the poetic contributions to the original, signed by such great masters of modern Russian poetry as Balmont, Bunin, Z. Hippius, Sologub, and Shchepkina-Kupernik.

My thanks are due to Dr. Louis S. Friedland and Professor Earle F. Palmer for going over a considerable portion of the present volume.

A. Yarmolinsky

Maxim Gorky – c.1906
Library of Congress Prints and Photographs Division
Washington, D.C. 20540 USA

Russia and the Jews

By Maxim Gorky

Alexey Maksimovich Pyeshkov, better known under
the assumed name of Maxim Gorky, was born in
1869. In 1905 he was arrested and imprisoned
because of his political convictions. After the revolutionary days of 1906 he left Russia and settled on
the island of Capri. At the beginning of the present
war he returned to Russia and took an active part
in the public life of the country. He is at present
residing in Petrograd, where he edits a monthly of
distinctly radical tendencies.

From time to time—more often as time goes
on!—circumstances force the Russian author
to remind his compatriots of certain indisputable, elementary truths.

It is a very hard duty:—it is painfully awkward to
speak to grown-up and literate people in this manner:

"Ladies and gentlemen! We must be humane; humaneness is not only beautiful, but also advantageous to us.
We must be just; justice is the foundation of culture. We
must make our own the ideas of law and civil liberty:
the usefulness of such an assimilation is clearly demon-

strated by the high degree of civilisation reached by the Western countries, for instance, by England.

"We must develop in ourselves a moral tidiness, and an aversion to all the manifestations of the brute principle in man, such as the wolfish, degrading hatred for people of other races. The hatred of the Jew is a beastlike, brute phenomenon; we must combat it in the interests of the quicker growth of social sentiments and social culture.

"The Jews are human beings, just like others, and, like all human beings, the Jews must be free.

"A man who meets all the duties of a citizen, thereby deserves to be given all the rights of citizenship.

"Every human being has an inalienable right to apply his energy in all the branches of industry and all the departments of culture, and the broader the scope of his personal and social activities, the more does his country gain in power and beauty."

There are a number of other equally elementary truths which should have long since sunk into the flesh and blood of Russian society, but which have not as yet done so.

I repeat—it is a hard thing to assume the role of a preacher of social proprieties and to keep reiterating to people: "It is not good, it is unworthy of you to live such a dirty, careless, savage life—wash yourselves!"

And in spite of all your love for men, in spite of your pity for them, you are sometimes congealed in cold despair and you think with animosity: "Where then is that celebrated, broad, beautiful Russian soul? So much was and is being said about it, but wherein does its breadth, might and beauty actively manifest itself? And is not our soul broad because it is amorphous?

And it is probably owing to its amorphousness that we yield so readily to external pressure, which disfigures us so rapidly and radically." We are good-natured, as we ourselves express it. But when you look closer at our good-naturedness, you find that it shows a strange resemblance to Oriental indifference.

One of man's most grievous crimes is indifference, inattention to his neighbour's fate; this indifference is pre-eminently ours.

The situation of the Jews in Russia, which is a disgrace to Russian culture, is one of the results of our carelessness, of our indifference to the straight and just decrees of life.

In the interests of reason, justice, civilisation, we must not tolerate that people without rights should live among us; we would never have tolerated it, if we had a strong sense of self-respect.

We have every reason to reckon the Jews among our friends; there are many things for which we must be grateful to them: they have done and are doing much good in those lines of endeavour in which the best Russian minds have been engaged. Nevertheless, without aversion or indignation, we bear a disgraceful stain on our consciousness, the stain of Jewish disabilities. There is in that stain the dirty poison of slanders and the tears and blood of numberless pogroms.

I am not able to speak of anti-Semitism in the manner it deserves. And this not because I have not the power or the right words. It is rather because I am hindered by something that I cannot overcome. I would find words biting, heavy, and pointed enough to fling them in the face of the man-haters, but for that purpose I must descend into a kind of filthy pit. I must put myself on a level with people whom I do not respect and for whom I have an organic aversion.

I am inclined to think that anti-Semitism is indisputable, just as leprosy and syphilis are, and that the world will be cured of this shameful disease only by culture, which sets us free, slowly but surely, from ailments and vices.

Of course, this does not relieve me of the duty to combat in every way the development of anti-Semitism and, according to my powers, to preserve people from getting infected by it. The Jew of to-day is dear to me, and I feel myself guilty before him, for I am one of those who tolerate the oppression of the Jewish nation, the great nation, whom some of the most prominent Western thinkers consider, as a psychical type, higher and more beautiful than the Russian.

I think that the judgment of these thinkers is correct. To my mind, Jews are more European than the Russians are, because of their strongly developed feeling of respect for work and man, if not for any other reason. I admire the spiritual steadfastness of the Jewish nation, its manly idealisms, its unconquerable faith in the victory of good over evil, in the possibility of happiness on earth.

The Jews—mankind's old, strong leaven,—have always exalted its spirit, bringing into the world restless, noble ideas, goading men to embark on a search for finer values.

All men are equal; the soil—is no one's, it is God's; man has the right and the power to resist his fate, and we may stand up even against God,—all this is written in the Jewish Bible, one of the world's best books. And the commandment of love for one's neighbour is also an ancient Jewish commandment, just as are all the rest, "thou shalt not kill" among them.

In 1885 the German-Jewish Union in Germany published "The Principles of the Jewish Moral Doctrine." Here is one of these principles: "Judaism teaches: 'Love thy neighbour as thyself' and announces this commandment of love for all mankind to be the fundamental principle of Jewish religion. It, therefore, forbids all kinds of hostility, envy, ill-will, and unkindly treatment of any one, without distinction of race, nationality and religion."

These principles were ratified by 350 rabbis, and published just at the time of the anti-Jewish pogroms in Russia.

"Judaism teaches respect for the life, the health, the forces and the property of one's neighbour."

I am a Russian. When, alone with myself, I calmly scrutinise my merits and demerits,—it seems to me that I am intensely Russian. And I am deeply convinced that there is much that we Russians can and ought to learn from the Jews.

For instance, the seventh paragraph of the "Principles of the Jewish Moral Doctrine" says: "Judaism commands us to respect work, to take part by either physical or mental labour in the communal work, to seek for life's goods in constant productive and creative work. Judaism, therefore, teaches us to take care of our powers and abilities, to perfect them and apply them actively. It, therefore, forbids all idle pleasure not based on labour, all idleness which hopes for the help of others."

This is beautiful and wise, and this is just what we Russians lack. Oh, if we could educate our unusual powers and abilities, if we had the will to apply them actively in our chaotic, untidy existence, which is terribly blocked up with all kinds of idle clack and home-spun philosophy, and which gets more and more saturated with silly arrogance and puerile bragging. Somewhere deep in the Russian soul—no matter whether it is the "master's" or the muzhik's—there lives a petty and squalid demon of passive anarchism, who infects us with a careless and indifferent attitude toward work, society, people, and ourselves.

I believe that the morality of Judaism would assist us greatly in overcoming this demon,—if only we have the will to combat him.

In my early youth I read—I have forgotten where—the words of the ancient Jewish sage—Hillel, if I remember rightly: "If thou art not for thyself, who will be for thee? But if thou art for thyself alone—wherefore art thou?" [1]

The inner meaning of these words impressed me with its profound wisdom, and I interpreted them for myself in this manner: I must actively take care of myself, that my life should be better, and I must not impose the care of myself on other people's shoulders; but if I am going to take care of myself alone, of nothing but my own personal life,—it will be useless, ugly and meaningless.

This thought ate its way deep into my soul, and I say now with conviction: Hillel's wisdom served me as a strong staff on my road, which was neither even nor easy. It is hard to say with precision to what one owes the fact that one kept on his feet on the entangled paths of life, when tossed by the tempests of mental despair, but I repeat—Hillel's serene wisdom assisted me many a time.

I believe that Jewish wisdom is more all-human and universal than any other, and this not only because of its immemorial age, not only because it is the first-born, but also because of the powerful humaneness that saturates it, because of its high estimate of man.

"The true Shekinah—is man," says a Jewish text. This thought I dearly love, this I consider the highest wisdom, for I am convinced of this: that until we learn to admire man as the most beautiful and marvellous phenomenon on our planet, until then we shall not be set free from the abomination and lies that saturate our lives.

It is with this conviction that I have entered the world, and with this conviction I shall leave it, and in leaving it I will believe firmly that the time will come when the world will acknowledge that

"The holy of holies is man!"

It is unbearably painful to see that human beings who have produced so much that is beautiful, wise and necessary for the world, live among us oppressed by unfair laws, which in all ways restrain their right to life, work and freedom. It is necessary,—for it is just and useful—to give the Jew equal rights with the Russians; it is imperative that we should do so not only out of respect to the people which has rendered and is constantly rendering yeoman service to humanity and our own nation, but also out of self-respect.

We must make haste with this plain, human reform, for the animosity against Jews is on the increase in our country, and if we do not make an attempt to arrest the growth of this blind hatred, it will prove pernicious to our cultural development. We must bear in mind that the Russian people have hitherto seen very little good, and therefore, believe all the evil things that man-haters whisper in their ears. The Russian peasant does not manifest any organic hatred for the Jew,—on the contrary, he shows an exceptional attraction for Israel's religious thought, fascinating for its democratic spirit. As far as I can remember, the religious sects of "judaizers" exist only in Russia and Hungary. In late years, the sects of "Sabbathists" and "The New Israel" have been developing rather rapidly in our country. In spite of this, when the Russian peasant hears of persecutions of Jews, he says with the indifference of an Oriental: "No one sues or beats an innocent man."

Who ought to know better than the Russian peasant that in "Holy Russia" the innocent are too often tried and beaten? But his conception of right and wrong has been confused from time immemorial, the sense of injustice is undeveloped in his dark mind, dimmed by centuries of Tartardom, boyardom, and the horrors of serfdom.

The village has a dislike for restless people, even when that restlessness is expressed in an aspiration for a better life. We Russians are intensely Oriental by nature, we love quiet and immobility, and a rebel, even if he be a Job, delights us in but an abstract way. Lost in the depth of a winter six months long, and wrapt in misty dreams, we love beautiful fairy-tales, but the desire for a beautiful life is undeveloped in us. And when on the plane of our lazy thought something new and disquieting makes its appearance,—instead of accepting and sympathetically scanning it, we hasten to drive it into a dark corner of our mind and bury it there, lest it disturb us in our customary vegetative existence, amidst impotent hopes and grey dreams.

In addition to the people, there is also the "populace," something standing outside of social classes and outside of culture, and united by the dark sense of hatred against everything surpassing its understanding and defenceless against brute force. I speak of the populace which thus defines itself in the words of Pushkin, our great poet, who himself suffered so cruelly from the aristocratic populace:

> "We are insidious and shameless,
> Ungrateful, faint-hearted and wicked;
> At heart we are cold, sterile eunuchs,
> Traducers, born to slavery."

It is mainly this populace that is the bearer of the brute principles, such as anti-Semitism.

The Jews are defenceless, and this is especially dangerous for them in the conditions of Russian life. Dostoyevsky, who knew the Russian soul so well, pointed out repeatedly that defencelessness arouses in it a sensuous inclination to cruelty and crime. In late years there have appeared in Russia quite a few people who have been taught to think that they are the finest of the wheat, and that their enemy is the stranger, above all—the Jew. For a long time these people were being persuaded that all the Jews are restless people, strikers and rioters. They were next informed that the Jews like to drink the blood of thievish boys. In our days they are being taught that the Polish Jews are spies and traitors.

If this preaching of hatred will not bring bloody and shameful fruits, it will be only because it will clash with our Russian indifference to life and will disappear in it;

it will split against the Chinese wall, behind which our still inexplicable nation is hidden. But if this indifference be stirred up by the efforts of the hatred preachers,—the Jews will loom up before the Russian nation as a race accused of all crimes.

And it is not for the first time that all the troubles of Russian life will be blamed on the Jew; time and again was he the scapegoat for our sins. Only recently he paid with his life and goods for the help he rendered us in our feverish struggle for freedom. I think no one has forgotten the fact that our "emancipatory movements" strangely wound up with anti-Jewish riots.

When the many-raced populace of Jerusalem demanded the death of the defenceless Jew, Christ, Pilate, believing Christ innocent, washed his hands, but allowed him to be put to death.

How then will honest Russian men and women act in Pilate's place? Their judgment is awaited.

Footnotes:
[1] "If I am not for myself who is for me? And being for my own self, what am I?" "Pirqe Aboth," I, 14.— Translator's Note.

The First Step

By Leonid Andreyev

Leonid Nikolayevich Andreyev, the author of impressive tales and remarkable dramas, is well known both in America and in England. Since the beginning of the Great War he has devoted himself to the artistic portrayal of the war's effect on his country, and also to purely publicistic tasks. He was born in 1871.

> "O heavens, if within your blue,
> Old God is still alive and mighty,
> Unseen by me alone, ye pray
> For me and for my doom e'er bleeding!
> My lips no more are fraught with hymns,
> No brawn in arm, no hope in heart....
> How long, how long, how long?"
> **—H. Byalik**

I t is with deep emotion that I have read in the Polish New Gazette an interview about the Jewish question with a personage of high station who seems to be really well informed. According to this personage, a number of measures are being proposed and planned, which are intended to lighten the grievous lot of the Jews in Russia: the abolition of the "Pale of Settlement" in relation to towns large and small, the abrogation of the percentage "norm" in the secondary and higher educational institutions, the establishment of special Jewish schools, the reorganisation of Jewish emigration on a broad and rational basis. I confess that I was not prompt in giving credence to these good tidings. And those with whom I shared the news, although excited no less than I, accepted them also with some degree of diffidence, which is only natural in Russians: life indulges us so rarely and so reluctantly. But private rumours corroborate this news, and to persist in one's disbelief would mean to doubt the very meaning of the present great "emancipatory" war, which is building a glorious temple of renovated life on the blood of Russians, Poles, Jews and Lithuanians. And finally, I simply cannot help believing, for my soul is weary with waiting and repeating together with the great Jewish poet: "How long, how long, how long?"

An aged journalist, who, it seems, has lost all fervour and faith, has recently laughed in his sleeve at the word "miracle," which nowadays comes so often to our lips: according to him, miracles, generally speaking, do not exist. It is my opinion also that there are no miracles, if we understand by a miracle an arbitrary violation of the natural, logical, inevitable order of things. But to him who contemplates life proper, not the table of multiplication,—logic itself appears as the greatest of all miracles. Oh, if logic would really reign supreme in life; oh, if in our cursed human existence, where there are so many aimless and unnecessary sorrows and tears and wild outrages, the simplest "two and two is four" would not be the rarest of miracles, equal to the transubstantiation of water into precious wine. Would

28

millions of individually innocent human beings perish in this most terrible of wars, if instead of a dark and terrible alogism a clear and lucid syllogism lay at the basis of our intricate and enigmatical existence? It is logic that is the true miracle, and "two and two is four" is that extraordinary happiness, which falls so seldom to our lot!

And just as I rejoiced as at miracles, at Russia's achievement of temperance, and Poland's rebirth in the same way, I now marvel at the coming solution of the "Jewish question," the immemorial and darkest of alogisms. There is something festive in it; it stirs up in me a feeling of serene and immense joy, bordering on religious exaltation.... And the fact that for me, as well as for many other Russian writers, all this was never even a problem, does not by any means diminish the extraordinary character of what is going to happen; for a plain brotherly kiss is almost a miracle and can move one to tears at the time when the rule of life and its highest wisdom is a fierce war of brother against brother.

And how can I help feeling this extraordinary import, I, a Russian intellectual, if, together with the solution of the "question" my soul, too, is suddenly set free. It is delivered from all the habitual and harrowing experiences that, constant companions of my days and nights as they have been, have acquired all the peculiarities of those chronic and incurable ailments, to which the grave alone can bring release. For, if to the Jews themselves the "Pale," the "norm," etc., were a fatal and impregnable fact, which deformed their entire life, they were also for me, a Russian, something in the nature of a hump on my back, a stationary and ugly growth, arising no one knows when or under what circumstances. Wherever I went and whatever I did, the hump was with me; at night it disturbed my sleep, and in my waking hours, when I was among people, it filled me with feelings of confusion and shame.

It is not my intention to demonstrate the soundness and justice of the proposed measures and to force the door which to me was always open, but I am going to take the liberty of adding a few more words about my hump. When did the "Jewish question" leap on my back?—I do not know. I was born with it and under it. From the very moment I assumed a conscious attitude towards life until this very day I have lived in its noisome atmosphere, breathed in the poisoned air which surrounds all these "problems," all these dark, harrowing alogisms, unbearable to the intellect.

Who needs it? Whom does it benefit? If all this exists and is supported, if there are people who assert it fiercely and firmly, there must be some definite sense in it; evidently, the Pale, the educational norm, and the rest increase mankind's sum of joy, exalt life, broaden the limits of human possibilities. Taking a logical point of departure, that is what I thought, but this same logic dictated to me an absolutely negative answer to all these questions: no one needs it, it brings good to no one: all these discriminations not only do not increase the sum of joy on this earth, but engender a multitude of wholly unnecessary, aimless sufferings; some they oppress, and others they badly corrupt. And yet I, a Russian intellectual, a happy representative of the sovereign race, although fully conscious and convinced that the "Jewish question" is no question at all,—I felt powerless and doomed to the most sterile tribulation of spirit.

For, all the clear-cut arguments of my intellect, the most fervent tirades and speeches, the sincerest tears of compassion and outcries of indignation unfailingly broke against a dull, unresponsive wall. But all powerlessness, if it is unable to prevent a crime, becomes complicity; and this was the result: personally guiltless of any offence against my brother, I have become in the eyes of all those unconcerned and those of my brother himself, a Cain.

The first consequence of my fatal powerlessness was that the Jew did not trust me, which meant that I lost my self-confidence. Living together with the Jews as my co-citizens, being in constant personal and business relations with them, in the field of consorted social work, I came face to face with the Jewish "problem" every single day,—and every single day of my life I felt with intolerable keenness all the falsehood and wretched ambiguity of my situation, that of an oppressor against one's will. In the doctor's office, at my desk, in the editorial room, in the street, finally in jail, where together with the Jew I fulfilled the all-Russian prison duty—everywhere I remained the privileged "Russian," the representative of the sovereign race, the baron,— without the baronial blazon. And with horror I noticed that even the eyes of a Jew-friend were dimmed with strange shadows ... that terrible images surged behind my friendly Russian shoulders and mingled wholly unsuitable noises and voices with my sincere plea for "world citizenship." ... And yet he knew me well, he knew my attitude toward the Jews,—how about those who know only that I am a "Russian"?

I remember having spent one night in talking with a very gifted writer, a Jew, who was my casual and most welcome guest. I was trying to convince him that he, a great master of the word, ought to write, but he repeated obstinately that although he loves the Russian language with all his artist's heart, he cannot write in it, in the language which has the word zhid. [1] Of course, logic was on my side, but on his side there was some dark truth—truth is not always lucid—and I felt, that my ardent arguments began, little by little, to sound like false and cheap babbling. So that I have not succeeded in convincing him, and when we parted I had not the courage to kiss him: how many unexpected meanings could be disclosed in this plain, everyday token of friendship and affection?

Things are altogether bad when even a kiss becomes suspicious and can be susceptible of "interpretation," as a complicated act of intricate and enigmatic relations! That is exactly what happened. And how many odd and nightmare-like misunderstandings were engendered by the poisonous mist in which we all wandered, both friends and foes, and in which the outlines of the plainest objects and feelings assumed the dismal grotesqueness of phantoms. I cannot help recalling here the case of E.A. Chirikov, which at the time excited much comment: the noble and fervent champion of the persecuted race, the author of the drama "Jews," which has more than any other Russian drama contributed to the dispersion of the evil prejudice,—this man was suddenly, in a most absurd manner, without a shadow of foundation, insulted by the accusation of anti-Semitism; and—to think of it!—it was necessary to furnish proofs that the accusation was false. What a painful, what a wholly disgraceful absurdity!

"Who needs all this? Who does not know it?" wearily thought every one of us, again and again realising the harrowing necessity of convincing some unbeliever, that two and two is four ... nothing but four!

And abroad? "What an injustice!"—thought I, when the cultured West, having separated me from Tolstoy, as if I had stolen him, handed me on the spot, a bill for the "excesses" known the world over, at the same time frowning unambiguously upon my eternal hump. The West refused to consider that I, too, am against this. I was considered a Russian, and the question was put this way: "Tell me, why in your country, in Russia?..."

It is ridiculous and utterly odd to think that our far-famed "barbarism" of which our enemies accuse us and which puts our friends out of countenance, is based wholly and exclusively on our Jewish question and its bloody excesses. Take away from Russia these excesses, leave, if you wish, the anti-Semitism, but in that externally decorous form in which it still exists in the backward portions of Europe,—and we shall become at once decent Europeans, and not Asiatics and barbarians, whose proper place is beyond the Ural. This is a fact the obviousness of which every new day of the present war makes more strikingly evident.

Of course culturally we are far behind the world, our economic life is undeveloped, our civic life is at a low level, and all the aspects of our life show clearly that we have not as yet broken the shell of the egg. But we are young, we are only beginning, and for a people who abolished serfdom only half a century ago, we have done quite a good deal,—so that, at the worst, lack of culture is the only reproach which a European with a sense of justice will fling at us. But it is enough to put side by side the words "Russian" and "Jew,"—and I become at once a barbarian, a dark and terrible being, who chills and darkens resplendent Europe. At once in America people begin to hate me, in England and France to despise me; with the swiftness of theatrical transformations Tolstoy's compatriot turns into the brother of those who drive nails into their neighbours' heads,—I become a barbarian. And even the German anti-Semite, a stupid and dull creature, looks down at me and warns England: "See with whom you are friends? Are they not the same people who...?"

"To whose interest is it that Europe should despise me, hate and fear me?" I mused, perplexed, feeling that in the light of the European sun my cursed hump assumes immense proportions and like a screen shuts off the light which comes from the East, and in which the aged and weary West is quite inclined to believe. To whom is it necessary for me to ramble among the cultured nations like a leper, to conceal my race and obtain the ironical bow so essential to my unacknowledged dignity, by means of exorbitant "tips" flung right and left? A barbarian, a barbarian!...

The war has opened our eyes to many things, and therein lies for us Russians the sad advantages of it. And now when Germany brands France and England for the union with "the Russian barbarians who...," when the allies, while relying on our elemental force, tremble with doubts and fear behind the screen of their noisy sympathies,—I begin to understand in whose interests it was, who needed it, that in the legion of European states we should remain all alone with our barbarism. Whatever is a misfortune for us is favourable for Germany, with her "well-tried" friendship for us, to which Wilhelm referred so loudly from the balcony of his palace. As barbarians we are only an excellent and indispensable market for the Germans' merchandise, a two-hundred-million flock of sheep ready for the shears. As a cultured nation we are a power dangerous to the Teuton's dream of world dominion. And the Jewish question, with its excesses and nails driven into heads, is that trump which our honest German neighbour has always kept hidden in his cuff and which he throws out on the green table at the necessary moment. And he was right from his standpoint. But why had we to drink off the bitter cup? Losing our self-respect, having no faith in our power, growing corrupted by an unnatural existence, cutting down by means of the celebrated "norm" the number of our educated and cultured men—a devilish joke!—our entire nation was diligently performing the "Fools' Dance," which, under the name of a drama from Russian life, has recently met with such a success in the Berlin playhouses. It must not be forgotten that the ardent Polish anti-Semitism, which frightens us so much and which seriously hinders the upbuilding of a new life, as well as the cold Finnish anti-Semitism, the power of which is still unknown to us,—that these two phenomena are nothing but the logical development of the fundamental absurdity, its natural and poisonous fruits. But the time has not come yet to speak about that.

May I be pardoned that in an hour so momentous for the Jews I persist in speaking not of them and their sufferings, but of ourselves. I repeat, the Jewish question was never a question for me, and in order to justify the proposed measures I need not allege the heroism shown by the Jews in defending Russia, their love for Russia, tragic in its faithfulness. As for demonstrating again and again that a Jew, too, is a human being, to do so would mean not only to bow too low to absurdity, but also to insult those whom I respect and love. And if I persist in speaking of ourselves and our suffering, it is not for personal egoism, nor even class egoism, but the pardonable egoism of a nation, which has been too long playing a miserable part on Europe's stage and in its own conscience, and which now repudiates the suffering of yesterday and, at the dawn of new life, seeks the possibility—oh, only the possibility!—of respecting itself.

Yes, we are still barbarians, the Poles still mistrust us, we are a dark terror for Europe, a baffling menace to her civilisation, but we do not want to be that any more, we long for purity and reason, our wretched rags burden us beyond all measure. The Jews' tragic love for Russia finds a counterpart in our love for Europe, as tragical in its faithfulness and completeness. Are we not ourselves the Jews of Europe, and is not our frontier—the same "Pale of Settlement"—something in the nature of a Russian Ghetto? And try as our Pushkin and Dostoyevsky and your Byalik may to prove that we, too, are human beings, people do not believe us, as they do not believe you: here is that equality whence we all can derive a bitter consolation; here is the punishment by means of which impartial life takes revenge on the Russians for the Jews' sufferings.

The thirst for self-respect—that is the fundamental feeling which now, in the days of the most terrible war, has seized all Russian society, which has exalted the people to the heights of heroism, and which makes us fear all that reminds us of our sad past. That is why persecution of Germans in our own country is so unbearable to us; we want no persecution; that is why we hate all that, like the belching of yesterday's drinking, distorts our disinterested aims and intentions: better yield than take too much of what belongs to other people—that is nowadays the motto of the majority. Could the country become sober if not for this feeling which one has when about to receive holy communion? Although proud at the victories of our arms, we scrupulously hide this pride, we treasure it in our hearts as our most precious possession, and we hate all swaggering and self-adulation. Not with the haughtiness of a righteous pharisee do we approach the altar, but with a prayer of penitence: "like a murderer I profess Thee."

We must all understand that the end of Jewish sufferings is the beginning of our self-respect, without which Russia cannot exist. The black days of war will pass, and the "German barbarians" of to-day will again become cultured Germans, to whose voice the world will once more hearken with deference. And we must never again allow this or any other voice to utter aloud: "The Russian barbarians."

Footnotes:
[1] This is an insulting synonym for "Jew."—Translator's Note.

Portrait of Vladimir Korolenko by Ilya Repin, 1912.
Oil on canvas. 75 × 64 cm.
The State Tretyakov Gallery, Moscow, Russia.

Mr. Jackson's Opinion on the Jewish Question

By Vladimir Korolenko

Vladimir Galaktionovich Korolenko is to-day universally recognized in Russia as the most worthy guardian of the best traditions of Russian letters. He has done yeoman service to his country both as an author of humanitarian tales and as the mouthpiece of Russia's public conscience. After the government some time ago suppressed the magazine "Russian Wealth" which Korolenko had edited, he retired to the city of Poltava, in the South, and in late years his appearance in print has been a rare event. He was born in 1853.

One of the most intelligent though not one of the most profound opinions about the Jewish question I happened to hear from a chance fellow-traveller on the Atlantic Ocean. And although it was quite some time ago, and the man who expressed it was in no way remarkable, nevertheless this opinion is recalled to me on various occasions—very frequently in these days.

It was in 1904. Together with a fellow countryman, also a man of letters, I was travelling aboard a steamer of the Anglo-American Company, "Cunard." Our cabin was small and narrow. It was lighted by the dull light of an electric bull's-eye in the ceiling which served as a deck. There were three berths and a wash basin. My friend and I occupied two of the berths. On the third there camped the gentleman about whom we read in the passenger list: "Mr. Henry Jackson of Illinois." This was all we knew about him for the first few days. He rose very early, went to bed late and spent all day outside of the cabin. As a rule, we woke early, because to the muffled and steady splash of the ocean over the sides of the ship there was added a splash issuing from the basin, nearby. By the dim light of the bull's-eye I could see from my top berth a tall figure in a nightshirt as long as a shroud, with a small bald spot on the pate. Out of delicacy he did not turn on the electric lights and in the semi-darkness made his toilet very quietly, but was not able to forego the pleasure of emitting some snorts while splashing himself with cold water from the basin. Then he dived again into his berth and for some time quietly and cautiously busied himself there; then—a light squeak of the door, and a long figure glided out from the cabin. We were interested in the personality of our neighbour. He was the first American whom fate had brought so near to us. We were unable even to distinguish his face and during the day tried to single him out in the international crowd of gentlemen scurrying about the deck of our Urania, lounging on the deck-chairs, having luncheon, or dinner or supper, or lost in the smoke of cigars in the smoking room. This elusiveness made the personality of the traveller puzzling and interesting, and we bestowed the title of "Our American" now on one, now on another of the middle-aged American gentlemen. Of course, we marked as candidates the more interesting and typical figures.

The Urania had been on the ocean for quite some time when my friend at last said to me: "I have found out which American is ours. Here he comes now. Look!"

Along the railing, a lanky gentleman and a short stout lady were coming toward us. I felt a sense of involuntary disappointment: both he and she were the least interesting of all the first-class passengers on the Urania.

A kind of half-European, half-exotic troupe were on the boat. They were going to America for a tour. The central figures in the group were two beautiful Creoles who had already succeeded in gaining a reputation in Europe. Around them were grouped a few stars of smaller magnitude, and the whole constellation attracted considerable attention from the men of the various nationalities represented on board. Soon a few couples circling the decks together came into notice. Amongst them were the lanky gentleman and the short, very vulgar lady, who looked like a maid or a duenna. As they passed in front of the other couples, one could sometimes notice slightly ironical glances and meaning smiles. But "our" American had a most self-satisfied, even somewhat victorious look. My companion, well-versed in English soon made a few acquaintances. Most often I saw him converse with "our" American in the hours when the latter was free from his knightly duties. Pretty soon we gained an insight into the main facts of his life-history. We learned that in his youth he had followed in turn a number of various callings, until one of them brought him success. He had retired and was now living on his large income, had provided very well for his two sons, had lost his wife, and decided to devote to pleasure the rest of his life which had begun amidst drudgery and many vicissitudes. He spent his time in travelling from one son to the other and retiring now and then to his own well-furnished home in Chicago. "When travelling you very often have very interesting adventures, don't you?" And he shot a triumphant and sly glance in the direction of his artistic lady.

Having learned that we were Russian writers, he decided at once that we were going to the Exhibition in the capacity of correspondents.

"Oh, yes, in my hard days I ate bread baked in this oven, too," he said, with an air of satisfaction. "There are many occupations which are more respectable and profitable.... But one tries everything. I can give you a good piece of advice. On the first train which will take you into the interior of the country, you will encounter a young man who offers illustrated guide-books for sale. Do not grudge your half-dollar, and buy these guide-books as frequently as possible. You will find in them excellent descriptions of noteworthy places, written by real masters. You can draw from them quite liberally. Even we, Americans, cannot know all our guide-books, as for Russia.... Heh-heh! Before reaching Chicago you will have several thousand lines.... Your readers will be satisfied, and so will your editor and you will earn your pay easily.... What?... Isn't that so?"

"Much obliged, sir!" answered my companion with ironical civility, and added in Russian: "The swine! He is cock-sure that he has benefited us highly by his advice."

My companion had a strong sense of humour, and every day he had some new episode, some characteristic opinion held by the American or some story of his past to tell me. Sometimes he would take out his note-book and make believe he was respectfully taking notes on some especially happy passages from these enlightening conversations. And at the same time he would say to me in Russian:

"He is deeply convinced that America is the best country in the world, Illinois is the best State in America, the street he lives on is the best street in his city, and his house the best house on the street. Now he is trying to persuade me that Chicago outgrew New York long ago and is now the first city in the world. Wait a minute ... there comes another one. That one is a New Yorker." He stopped the gentleman who was passing by and proceeded to introduce them to each other: "Mr. Jackson of Illinois, Mr. Carson of New York." Then in the naïve tone of a person, somewhat perplexed, he asked: "You told me that New York is the first city in the world. And here is Mr. Jackson who asserts that for the last ten years Chicago has outstripped New York in population. According to him Chicago has so many million inhabitants."

My companion leaned back slightly in his arm-chair and looked with obvious curiosity at the two Americans. "Presently we shall have a cock-fight," he said to me in Russian, and a mocking twitch appeared beneath his moustache.

Mr. Carson straightened up. His eyebrows lifted impatiently but immediately his face took on an expression of polite calm, and slightly tipping his hat, he said: "It is very possible ... the gentleman evidently includes the population of the cemeteries of Chicago." He bowed and resumed his walking, leaving Mr. Jackson aghast with mouth wide-open, speechless, for he had not time to protest. Then he got up quickly and walked along the deck.... My companion followed him with his smiling eyes....

"Perfect parrots," he said. "Petty patriotism, in its most naïve form.... Dickens long ago noticed that trait of American character and so it goes on." My sly countryman skilfully interviewed his victim, disclosing step by step the ludicrous traits of a Yankee. There were many weak sides. Mr. Jackson, in whom we were mainly interested, proved to be a mediocre person in all respects, with a naïvely middle-class outlook on life, and we, the two Russian observers, revelled in that delightful malice which is so characteristic of Russians abroad. So that is what they are, the far-famed children of the transatlantic republic!

Sometime later, I again found my companion engaged in conversation with Mr. Jackson. The ocean was somewhat rough. The ladies did not come out on deck; Mr. Jackson was, therefore, free and evidently in high spirits. He spoke with great animation. My companion had his note-book in his hands and there was a slyly respectful smile on his face.

"We are discussing the Jewish question," he said in Russian. "Mr. Carson, a quarter of an hour ago, praised the Jews, and ever since 'our man' cannot calm down. He enlightens me with arguments which sound as if they were just taken from our yellow newspapers. Please, go on, sir," he respectfully addressed Mr. Jackson. "Everything you say is so new and interesting...."

Mr. Jackson, who was flattered by the respectful attention of the naïve Russian, continued his sermon. It was before the days of the Beyliss trial. Nevertheless, except for the "ritual" murder, all the rest of the jargon

44

of our anti-Semitic papers was there, and the Jewish character was painted the most frightful black.

On the other end of the deck resounded the shrill sound of the gong, a signal for lunch.

"Thank you, sir," said my companion. "It is with great pleasure that I have listened to your views on the subject, and I am certain that all this will be found extremely novel in our country.... I have a few more minutes to ask you one last question...."

"What else do you wish to know?" said Mr. Jackson.

"I wonder," answered my friend, "what conclusions are to be drawn from this enlightening conversation. You are undoubtedly against equal rights for the Jews. You would shut the doors of the country for the Jews, wouldn't you? And you would limit the rights of those who already live there, by establishing, let us say, something in the nature of a special zone outside of which they would not be allowed to settle?"

Even as my friend was saying this the American's eyebrows went up, forming a sharp angle, and he looked at the speaker with such an air of pity that the latter was somewhat put out of countenance.

"How in the world have you reached such a conclusion?" asked Jackson coldly, and somewhat severely.

"But ... you dislike the Jews heartily...."

The clanging of the gong was reaching our corner. Mr. Jackson rose and buttoning his coat, he said: "It does

STOP YOUR CRUE

ROOSEVELT (*to the czar*)—" Now that you have peace

Theodore Roosevelt to the Emperor of Russia, Nicholas II, "Now that you have peace without, why not remove his burden and have peace within your borders?"

46

ON OF THE JEWS.
ove his burden and have peace within your borders?"

By Emil Flohri. C. 1904.
Library of Congress Prints and Photographs Division
Washington, D.C. 20540 USA

not follow. You have made a bad syllogism: the conclusion does not follow from the premises."

"But, sir...."

"It is true that I dislike those people, but it doesn't follow that I want their rights restricted...."

And after a moment of deliberation, as though seeking for the clearest form of explanation, he went on.

"Here we are being called for dinner ... I must tell you, sir, that I cannot tolerate green peas. That is my personal taste. But it does not follow by any means, gentlemen, that I have the right to demand that green peas should not be served.... Probably, others like the dish...."

And rising to his full height, he added: "As for the rest of your words ... as an American, I would feel insulted, if there were in my country citizens deprived of equal rights.... That a Kentuckian, for instance, should not have the right to breathe freely the air of Illinois.... My goodness.... The idea!"

And he started out, moving along the railing, straight and gaunt, and, there was something peculiar in his entire figure. He seemed to feel himself deeply insulted. At the door of the smoking-room, he met Mr. Carson of New York, his recent antagonist, and amiably taking his arm, he started to tell him something in great excitement. Judging by the way Mr. Carson turned to look at us, it was evident that they were discussing us Russians, the gentlemen who draw false conclusions from premises.

We exchanged glances. Half a minute passed in perplexed silence. Then we both laughed at once....

"Rira bien qui rira le dernier. We must confess that this time it is 'our' rather bad American who laughs last," said my sarcastic friend. "And did you notice the expression on his face at that moment?"

"Yes, it looked positively intelligent.... Probably, because the experience and wisdom of a great nation, which has already firmly established axioms, were speaking at that moment through the mouth of our American...."

"And the negroes?" said my friend hesitatingly and thoughtfully.

"Well, the negroes are 'the black peas' which Americans detest. But that is a matter of social custom; the law, however, does not distinguish them from other citizens.... To love, not to love ... that is elusive and capricious, but justice is obligatory, like an axiom...."

Entering the dining-room, I felt somewhat uneasy.... It seemed to me that all the Americans would turn and eye us, the representatives of a nation which has not as yet learned the axioms of law, and which draws childishly false conclusions from premises....

But I was mistaken. There was in the dining-room the usual rustling, clatter of plates, forks and knives, tinkling of glasses, and whispered conversation. "Our" American was sitting at the side of his odd Dulcinea, and he again looked like a self-satisfied cox-comb. But, it seemed to me that into the everyday mood of the vessel's table-d'hôte, there entered something elusive and significant, which could change the appearance of this motley crowd just as our American's face had changed at the end of our conversation.

And, in fact, a few weeks later, I happened to be present at one of those tempestuous manifestations of public opinion which at times break out like storms on the surface of the ocean. There is much that is ridiculous in the every-day tone of American newspapers, in their thirst for sensations and réclame, in their petty interviews. But here everything was suddenly swept aside, and the dominant tone of the American press became deep and significant. Now and then the voices of past generations,—the men who had been the builders of freedom and law in their country, the voices of Lincolns, Harrisons, and Davises pierced the bustle of every-day life and were heard in editorials, articles, in the speeches delivered at meetings.

The occasion for all this was again the Jewish question, and the ignorance of axioms shown by a nation of the old continent. And it occurred to me that probably somewhere in Chicago, Mr. Jackson, "who dislikes green peas," was delivering, or at least listening to, a speech about the axioms of human law, and was voting in favor of a corresponding resolution.

For he firmly believes that love is capricious. Like mercy, it bloweth, whither it listeth.... But justice, justice is obligatory....

The Jewish Question in Russia

By P. Milyukov

Professor Paul Nikolayevich Milyukov, the central figure in the present Russian revolution, was born in 1859. Before the upheaval in 1905 he was known as a distinguished historian. In 1903 and 1904 he lectured on Russia at Harvard and at the University of Chicago, and in 1908 he spoke on the situation in Russia before the Civic Forum in Carnegie Hall. Ever since the revolutionary days of 1905-6, Professor Milyukov has been playing a most conspicuous part in the Russian emancipatory movement, as the leader of the Constitutional party, as a Duma deputy and the editor of the influential radical newspaper Ryech.

The Jewish question in Russia presents altogether peculiar aspects. This is not only because there are in the Empire six million Jews, i.e., more than in any other State in the world, and because in the provinces annexed at the end of the eighteenth and the beginning of the nineteenth centuries, they form as much as 11 per cent of the population—but also for the reason that the legal status of the Russian Jews completely differs from that of other non-Russian nationalities which go to make the Empire. These nationalities endeavour to obtain the many rights of which they are deprived. The most important of these rights is national autonomy, i.e., the right of a collective unit to preserve and develop its national individuality. In this manner they desire to protect themselves from the danger of assimilation, from the possibility of their fusion with the dominant nationality. Of course the Jews, too, have been striving, especially in late years, to realise national autonomy and thus safeguard the rights and aspirations of their collective unit. But they lack still other rights. They have still to be granted those rights which to a considerable degree other Russian subjects, not of Russian birth, enjoy. The law does not protect the elementary civil rights of the Jews as members of our common Russian commonwealth. Consequently, that which the Jews strive for is far more elementary, far more primitive and simple, than the objective of other non-Russian nationalities which inhabit Russia.

Anti-Semitism is not peculiar to Russia; it is to be found in other countries as well. But there it exists as an emotion and a state of mind, not as a system of legislative definitions. The time has long since passed when the legislatures of the world failed to guarantee the elementary civil rights of the Jews. Roumania alone constitutes a peculiar exception. But, as a rule, in all civilised States the law guarantees Jewish rights, and religious and racial differences do not create legal disabilities. Nevertheless, if anti-Semitism is still in existence in the Western countries, the aims it pursues there are political. It continues to be the weapon of political reaction. And its objective, at its extreme, is by no means like the grandiose programme of utter destruction of the Jews which is pursued by the "truly-Russian" theoreticians of our reaction.

Consequently, the Jewish question in Russia means, above all, the legal disabilities of the individual Jews that result from the discriminations made against them as a religious and national entity. It is only one aspect of our general inequality and of our lack of civil freedom. The problem of Jewish equal rights in Russia is the problem of the equal rights of all our citizens in general. That is why the anti-Semitical parties in Russia have a larger political significance and importance than the anti-Semitical parties of the West. In our country they almost coincide with anti-constitutional parties, in general, and anti-Semitism is the banner of the old regime, of which we still struggle in vain to rid ourselves. This accounts for the fact that the Jewish question occupies such a prominent place in Russian social and political life. Here the struggle for general rights coincides with the struggle for national rights. That is why the Jewish problem has come to occupy the centre of our political stage.

I must add that Russian anti-Semitism, as defined above, is a comparatively new phenomenon, in fact, it may be asserted that it is a phenomenon of most recent origin. However ancient may be the instincts on which our anti-Semites try to play, anti-Semitism itself as a political motto, as a movement with a party platform and definite aims, is a new means of political struggle, invented and applied only in late years. Of course, in the past there can be found manifestations—very crude and coarse—of what might be termed "zoological" anti-Semitism. In 1563, Ivan the Terrible conquered Polotzk, and for the first time the Russian Government was confronted by the fact of the existence of the Jewish nationality. The Czar's advisers were somewhat perplexed and asked him what to do with these newly acquired subjects. Ivan the Terrible answered unhesitatingly: "Baptise them or drown them in the river."

They were drowned. And the old Russian "zoological" nationalism was satisfied by this primitive solution of the problem. But the political wisdom of Czar Ivan's times has long since become obsolete.

A century later Russian statehood for the second time ran across the Jewish problem when Smolensk was taken by Czar Alexey Mikhaylovich the Debonnaire, also an old Russian nationalist who was not conscious of his nationalism. He could not make up his mind to settle it by simply destroying the object which perplexed Russia's political mind. After due deliberation, he decided to have the Jews deported. This was a somewhat milder measure. Another century passed, and Russia conquered the vast and rich territory which is included in the so-called "Pale of Settlement." This portion of Russia was peopled with many millions of Jews. It was not possible any longer to do away with this large population by either drowning it in a river, or even—as many are still planning in all earnestness—by deportation. Thus, the Russian state, in the person of Empress Catherine II, for the first time found itself forced to face the Jewish question in a form which did not allow of simply waving it aside. How then did the enlightened Empress settle it? Well, she simply did not put the question. Her decision was nearly this: The Jews have lived there—let them stay there; they had certain rights relating to their faith and property—let them enjoy these rights in the future. The Interpretation of the Senate even more strongly emphasised this thought. Here is the gist of this Interpretation: "Since the Imperial Ukase has placed the Jews in a legal status of equality with the rest of the population, the rule established by her Majesty should, therefore, be followed in application to each particular case. Every one should enjoy his rights and acquisitions according to his condition and calling without distinction of faith and nationality."

Such was the decision of the Senate of the time of Catherine the Great. There can be no question here of a negative solution of the Jewish problem, for the very possibility of such a problem was not considered. Least of all did Catherine think that in the lapse of years her ukase of December 23, 1791, in which neither faith nor nationality was mentioned, would give birth to ... the "Pale of Settlement." At that time the Jews were confined within the limits of the "Pale" neither more nor less than the Ukrainian population of that section, or the people of the old Russian provinces were. It will be remembered that in those times the law forbade a townsman to take up his residence in another town or in a village. It was not a special limitation intended for the Jews, it affected all the Russian subjects throughout the Empire. How then did it result in a special Jewish disability?

It did not result either from the increase in the rights of other citizens, or from the limitation of the rights of the Jews as a nationality. The afore-mentioned limitations were removed from the townspeople of non-Jewish birth both in the newly annexed provinces and elsewhere. But they remained in full force in relation to the Jews, living in towns. But since all the Jews were registered as townspeople, this restriction coincided with the limits of their nationality. Hence arose the "Pale" which assumed the character of a national disability. Thus, the problem of Jewish disabilities was practically solved before the legislator ever formulated the Jewish question.

For this reason, in the times of Catherine II, when the main features of the future Jewish disabilities were becoming a fact, the Government did not solve the general Jewish question in principle. Likewise, during the entire century which followed Catherine's reign, that is, all through the nineteenth century, our legislation was in a state of constant indecision.

A brief historical survey will show plainly the accuracy of this statement. In 1795 the Jews who lived in the villages of the Province of Minsk were ordered to move to the towns. In the following year they were permitted to stay in the villages, because the landed proprietors employed them as agents for the sale of whiskey. In the year 1801 a new edict again expels the Jews from the villages. In 1802 the Senate rules that they must stay in their former places of residence. In 1804—the year that saw the first Regulation concerning the Jews—they are ordered to be expelled within three years from the villages throughout the country. But in 1808 before the term expires the law is found impracticable. The Jews again remained where they had been established, their status being subject to further regulation. Then the Committee of the year 1812 came to the conclusion that the law of 1804 must be completely abrogated, in view of its being unjust and dangerous. Between 1812 and 1827 the mood of the legislation is again altered and prohibitive measures follow one another. In 1835, these measures are once more found to be useless and

56

inefficient. In 1852, expulsions are renewed, but a few years later, with the beginning of the liberal reign of Alexander II, this policy is again abandoned and an interval of rest and quiet, covering a quarter of a century, is inaugurated. Then the temporary Regulations of 1882 undertake to prohibit new Jewish settlements outside of towns. Former settlements, although illegal, were legalised and exempted from persecution. But in 1893 all the Jews who had illegally settled in the villages were again ordered to be expelled therefrom. Nevertheless, the committee of the year 1899 not only refused to ratify this measure, but, on the contrary, it recognised the necessity of relaxing even the old Temporary Regulation of 1882. And, in fact, in 1903 we find the Jewish settlements in 158 villages. At the same time, the Jewish rural population within the limits of the "Pale of Settlement" grew considerably. In 1881 there lived in the villages 580,000 Jews; in the year 1897 they reached the number of 711,000.

Thus did our legislation concerning the Jews fluctuate and vacillate. And amidst these hesitations the thought of a complete removal of all the Jewish disabilities never died. Here is another historical excursion covering a century. The Committee of Jewish Affairs of the year 1803 plainly established this regulation: "the maximum of freedom and the minimum of limitations." The second Committee, whose activities fall in the period from 1807 to 1812, proved even more thoroughgoing, for it was more familiar with the conditions of Russian life. It asserted that the Jews are useful and necessary for the Russian village. It added, furthermore, that the negative, dark phenomena which are attributed by some to the presence of Jews in the villages, in reality are characteristic of Russian life in general, and cannot be said to be due to the Jewish influence. This was also the opinion of the minority of the Imperial Council in 1835. In 1858, the Minister of the Interior himself demanded equal rights for the Jews, and the reactionary Committee on Jewish affairs agreed to the demand on the sole condition that the disabilities should be removed gradually, from various Jewish groups. The new Committee of 1872 acted even more vigorously. It believed that the abolition of Jewish disabilities is, in general, nothing but an act of justice, and that this abolition must be carried out not gradually, but immediately i.e. it must include all the groups of the Jewish population. Again, the Committee of 1883 comes to the same conclusion that it is necessary to give the Jews equal rights. That was the opinion even of Von Pleve, who is known to the world for his persecution of the Jews. In the period from 1905 to 1907 the revision of the legislation concerning the Jews for the purpose of abolishing the prohibitive measures was considered but a question of time and was left to the consideration of the people's representatives in the Imperial Duma which had just come into being. The opinion of the first two sessions of the Duma is well known. The People's representatives in the first two Dumas announced directly and unambiguously that the realisation of full civic freedom, for Jews as well as for the rest of the citizens, was one of their first tasks. Then a new reactionary election law was introduced. It made a radical change in the composition of the Imperial Duma and also in the attitude of the latter toward the Jewish question. The outright usefulness of the part played by the Jews in the economic life of both town and village,—this fact, which even reactionary governments, ministers and committees ceased doubting, was again questioned by the newly elected representatives of the Russian people. It is only from that moment on that it became possible to plan such measures as the abolition of those meagre rights which the Jews are still enjoying. Thus, together with the victory of political reaction the new anti-Semitism, which we cannot any longer over-look, has become triumphant.

Our historical excursion enables us also to explain the reason why in the present phrase of Russian social life the Jewish problem has again arisen in an unprecedented form. It was simply a new political weapon, in a sense, the result of the new form of political life. As long as the nation was voiceless, as long as all matters were decided by the bureaucracy in the quiet of offices, committees, and ministries, it was possible for the Government to ignore the people as a factor in legislation, and to take into account nothing but the needs and the welfare of the state as it understood them. But when the nation was called to participate in state affairs, there arose the need of influencing it in a certain sense. It became necessary to work up the masses, to act on their intellect and will. Official anti-Semitism is the most primitive means of satisfying this need, a simplified attempt to bridle the masses, to suggest to them the feelings, motives, views and methods which are in the interest of those who play the game. In other words, demagogy came into being. For the purposes of demagogy a special political weapon, corresponding to the political conditions under the new regime, was created,—namely artificial political parties.

Thus, anti-Semitism of the new type, however strange this conclusion may appear, is the product of the constitutional epoch. It is a response to the need for new means of influencing the masses. And in this sense anti-Semitism plays in Russia the same role as it played in Western Europe.

Bismarck, it will be remembered, called anti-Semitism the socialism of fools. In order to combat the socialism of intelligent people, it is necessary to take hold of the ignorant masses and to mislead them by showing them the imaginary enemy of their welfare instead of the real one. Anti-Semitism says to the ignorant masses: "There is your enemy, fight the Jews, and you will improve your life conditions...." It is well known that such attempts to apply anti-Semitism for the purpose of creating social parties of the new type were more than once made in the West. As an example, I shall cite the Christian Social Party in Austria, with its late leader, Lueger.

There is one small difference between us and the West. In Russia the masses are not so well prepared to appreciate a social argument, even when served in a simplified form. In Russia anti-Semitism is forced to present this argument in an even more popular form, making an appeal to the most elementary passions and instincts. F.I. Rodichev once remarked in the Duma, parodying Bismarck's aphorism to fit it to our conditions, that anti-Semitism is "the patriotism of perplexed people." In fact, anti-Semitism in Russia is a means of creating a nationalism of a definite type in the masses, it is with this aim in view that our anti-Semites play on the racial and religious animosities of the masses.

In spite of this difference, the very means, ways, and methods our anti-Semites use in their striving to mould the popular mind are of distinctly foreign origin. It is enough to collate the arguments expounded in the Duma or printed in the Russian Standard and Zemshchina with the anti-Semitic literature of the West, such as Drumont's books, or similar German works,—and it becomes apparent that in the latter the entire anti-Semitic arsenal of our nationalists is to be found ready-made. It is from thence that medieval legends of ritual murders and law projects concerning the slaughter of cattle, and such-like inventions, are imported to us.

Anti-Semitism serves in Russia one more purpose. It is not sufficient to influence the masses. It is also necessary to act on the powers that be. If it is imperative to get hold of the masses, it is also necessary to frighten the authorities. Thus a new version of the anti-Semitic legend comes into being: the legend of the Jew as the creator of the Russian revolution. It is the Jew,—so our anti-Semites assure us—who created the Russian emancipatory movements, it is he who formed the revolutionary organisation, it is he who marched under the red banners…. The Russian who would give credence to this tale would show his disrespect for the Russian nation. To assert that it is only owing to the help of the Jew that the Russian people freed themselves is tantamount to saying that without the Jew, the Russian nation can not reach the road of its own emancipation. No, however great my respect for the exceptional gifts of the Jewish people may be, I will not refuse the

Russian nation the ability of taking the initiative in the cause of its own freedom.

But there is another side to this matter. If there can be no question of the dependence of the emancipation movement on the Jews, the dependence of the Jews on the emancipatory movement is very real. What must be the Jew's attitude toward this movement? There can be only one answer to the question. The Jewish masses have realised the importance for them of the emancipatory movement not only because they are more enlightened, because they are more educated, because they are not addicted to alcoholism, and, hence, are superior to their neighbours in their understanding of their own needs; the Jewish masses were also led to side with the movement for freedom because in their case it was a struggle for elementary rights the importance of which is plain to every one and vitally concerns every one. That is why the entire Jewish mass may actually be reckoned in the ranks of those who are with the Russian emancipatory movement.

One more remark in conclusion. In late years the "inorodtzy" (Russian subjects of non-Russian birth), having lost their hope that the Russian emancipatory movement would bring them any immediate practical results, have sought to influence the Government by means of more direct methods. There are national movements which believe that they would more rapidly get national rights by means of negotiating with the bureaucracy. They are inclined to think that this way is more direct than the participation in the Russian emancipatory movement. Other national groups, in the struggle for their national rights, choose a different kind of tactics: they seek a more direct way in another direction,—not through the bureaucracy, not from above, but from below. They, too, believe that the "inorodtzy" must organise for their specific national aims and keep apart from the common cause of Russia's political emancipation.

From what has been said about the peculiar nature of the Jewish question which results in the sufferings of the Jews not only as a national group, but also as individual citizens, it follows that it is difficult for the Jews more than for any other group of "inorodtzy" to accept either one of the aforenamed tactical methods. The Jews must bear in mind with especial clearness that their fate is closely and inseparably interwoven with the fate of the general emancipatory movement in Russia. They must also keep in mind that the separate national movements which disrupt the bonds of political parties in order to make place for their national programmes, may prove injurious to our common cause. They may lead us away from the common highroad to by-paths where we all run the risk of going apart and losing our way. And here is the practical conclusion to which these considerations lead. The separate national movements should be postponed until the solution of the general problem of all-Russian emancipation. Let us hope that the Jewish nation understands the close connection existing between its fate and that of Russia's freedom, now, as well as it did in those years when it fought in the ranks of the Russian progressive movements. Let us hope that in the future, as in the past, the emancipation of the different nationalities which people the Russian Empire will be fought for in the common ranks of the all-Russian movement for freedom.

Jewish school children with a teacher.
Sergey Prokudin-Gorskii Collection (between 1905 and 1915).
Library of Congress, Washington, D.C. 20540 USA

The Jews and Russian Economic Life

By M. Bernatzky

Mikhail Vladimirovich Bernatzky, born in 1878, is a noted writer on economical topics. He taught economics at the Kiev University and at the Polytechnical Institute, Petrograd.

Much has been written about the insufferable situation of the Russian Jews, these serfs of the twentieth century, chained to "the Pale of Settlement," somewhat like the Roman colons, "glebae adscripti." The tragic history of late years and the epoch through which we are living can disturb the inner composure of the most indifferent spectator of current events. It is painful to touch upon many aching and essentially clear questions, but life constantly and severely demands that they should be brought before our minds, and life awaits an answer to them from the thought and conscience of Russian society.

It is not our intention to discuss the necessity for the removal of Jewish disabilities from the humanitarian standpoint. However majestic may be those "elementary principles of law and morality," which have been achieved by mankind on its long historic road and which are now the very basis of civilisation, in the eyes of many they are still little more than "fine words," stylistic embellishments of highbrow talk. Of course, the atmosphere of discriminations is equally pernicious for those who suffer and those who are privileged: did not serfdom corrupt the master as well as the slave? All this is eminently true. But there are arguments, which we regret to say, are more appealing and convincing. It is these arguments that we shall treat in the present paper.

The reader is well aware of the fact that in these days nothing has been discussed more vividly than the necessity of developing Russia's productive powers. The intimate connection between the general prosperity of our country and its economic progress has penetrated into the consciousness of people at large. It is the war, evidently, that has driven this truth home to us: namely that the ultimate success of the conflict depends not only on the activity of the armies, but also on the economic stability of the belligerent nations. The economic difficulties which are being experienced by Germany, strengthen our faith in our final victory. More than a quarter of a century ago the Russian Minister of Finance, who took great pains to develop our industry, wrote in the explanatory memoir which accompanied the project of the state budget: "I believe it to be the duty I owe Your Imperial Majesty to express my firm, clear, and profound conviction that economic prosperity of the people even when coupled with a somewhat imperfect military organisation will be more useful in case of war than the most complete military preparedness combined with economic weakness. In the latter case, the people, however eager they may be to sacrifice both their life and property, can bring to the altar of the fatherland their life only, but they will be unable to furnish the necessary financial means for the State."

It is from this standpoint of economic interests that we shall approach the painful Jewish question. The time is long since past when it was possible to say with the Empress Elizabeth Petrovna: "From Christ's enemies I desire no profit." It is precisely in this profit that both the Exchequer and the higher classes, and—what is most important—the people at large, are greatly interested. The basic productive force of a country is the living work of its population. The body politic of Russia contains about six millions of gifted and undoubtedly industrious Jews. The manner in which the forces of this people are applied will be treated further on. For the moment let us state this: it is to the interest of the Russian State to utilise economically this living Jewish energy as completely and rationally as possible. From this standpoint all the obstacles which are created for the Jews in the field of education are absolutely incomprehensible: it is as if our country, sorely lacking as it is not only in representatives of superior qualified labour, but actually in literate people, were striving to increase its ignorance and intellectual backwardness. Of course, formal justification can be found for every act, and every evil-doer endeavours to convince himself of the justice of his evil deeds. So it is in this case, too: the intentional shutting-off of the Jewish masses from education is motivated by the desire to keep them from becoming superior to the Russian population, which, it is said, is intellectually inferior to the Jews. This argument is an outright insult flung in the face of the Russian people. It shows that the official guardians of the nation do not know its rich natural powers. But this argument cannot obscure the essential nature of Jewish disabilities as an intentional neglect of that productive power which is represented by a portion of the Russian subjects. Our economic organism does not get all the benefits to which it may rightfully lay claim.

Let us turn to those characteristic social and economic conditions under which the Jews exist in our country. Nearly all of them, upward of five millions, live within the Pale of Settlement, which comprises fifteen governments and Poland, and only six per cent live outside of this territory. Within the Pale, Jews are not allowed to buy or take on lease real estate outside the towns and townlets, which circumstance makes it impossible for them to become farmers. This, in connection with the limitation of residence, has naturally resulted in a peculiar character of the Jewish occupations. It is characteristic of the part the Jews play in Russia's economic life that nearly seventy-three and eight hundredths per cent of them are forced to seek employment in the country's commerce and industry. Of the entire Jewish population throughout the Empire, only two and four tenths per cent are engaged in agriculture, four and seven tenths per cent in liberal professions, eleven and five tenths per cent in personal service (domestic service etc.); the rest, minus the persons without any definite employment are forced to seek for means of livelihood in the field of commerce (thirty-one per cent), industry (thirty-six and three tenths per cent), and transport (three per cent) In the same way works the artificial congestion of the Jews in the cities: only eighteen per cent live in the villages of the Pale of Settlement, while the rest—more than four-fifths—toil in the towns and townlets. Such a one-sided distribution of Jewish labour would not be a negative phenomenon if it were possible to spread it uniformly over the entire country. For, backward as Russia is industrially and commercially, the Jews would easily find a place in the fields of endeavour which suit them best and would greatly benefit the country by furthering the process of its industrialisation. Under present circumstances they are crowded in one place and overburden the commerce and the industry of the Pale of Settlement. As a result, the struggle for existence among them is so keen and desperate that in some sections they are undoubtedly on the way to degeneration. In the West, Galicia and Roumania excluded, the Jews are well represented in the wealthy classes; in Russia an overwhelming portion of them are proletaries, "free like birds," poverty-stricken people who literally do not know to-day by what they are going to live to-morrow. Heart-rending pictures are painted by impartial observers of the life of the Jewish poorer classes, of all these tradesmen, factory workers, petty merchants and peddlers. They literally starve and cripple both mind and body in the slums of cities and towns. The natural result is that in their eager search for means of livelihood they are forced to have recourse to all sorts of expedients. Hence, all this talk about the "criminal features" of the Jewish character and their propensity for financial speculation, which propensity is, however, easily forgiven and even encouraged in the "true-Russian" representatives of our commercial interests. On the other hand, the Jews lower "the standards of living" by offering their services often at a very low price. Thus a peculiar "social anti-Semitism" comes into being, in Russia as well as in the countries of Jewish immigration,—a phenomenon not unlike the movement against "yellow labour" in the United States and in the Australian Federation. There can be no doubt that the artificially restrained field of application of Jewish labour is alone responsible for the unspeakable condition in which it is forced to exist. In spite of the exodus of a large mass of Jews from Russia, which bears analogy to the emigration of the Irish people from their native country,—upward of one and a half million Jews left Russia between the years 1881 and 1908,—the remaining millions seem to be doomed to starvation and degeneration. The popular tales about Jewish wealth are most emphatically contradicted by impartial facts. Of the emigrants who reach the shores of America the Jews are the poorest. A Scotch emigrant coming to the United States brings on the average $41.50, an Englishman $38.70, a Frenchman $37.80, a German $28.50, while a Jew brings the sum of $8.70, the smallest of all, far below the general average, which is $15.00. Consequently, if any real danger at all threatens the aboriginal Russian population, it is precisely the cheap labour of the congested Jewish masses, and the more the Jews will be oppressed the worse it will be for the Russian workman! For the employer will always give preference to cheaper labour. It is evident, therefore, that the present treatment of the Jews is really not dictated by the native Russian population, and that the democratic argument is but a false pretext. The Russian labour market, while congested in the Pale, is scarce in other sections. That the economic life of Russia, as a whole, suffers from it is obvious.

In this connection, another point is worthy of our attention. Contrary, to the popular idea of the Jewish greed, the Jews are usually satisfied with a lower rate of interest on the capital invested, since what they are after is the bare means of livelihood. In this fashion they lower, to a considerable extent, the capitalist's profits, a circumstance which cannot fail to irritate the Gentile capitalists. Consequently, all this comes to competition of capital, and it is significant that the fiercest anti-Semitic outcries come from the capitalistic classes. Let us not forget that the early pogroms at Odessa were caused by the agitation of the Greek merchants who feared for their commercial ascendency.

What has been said so far demonstrates with sufficient clearness that the anti-Semitic economic policy is detrimental to the economic organism of Russia as a whole. The true interests of our country demand that Jewish labour and Jewish means should be given complete freedom of application. Russia will only gain from such a change of policy toward the Jews. Anti-Semitism, from the economic standpoint, is nothing but a tremendous waste of the country's productive powers.

Here is another aspect of the question. Whether the Jews as a race are to one's liking or not, is a question of individual taste, the solution of which cannot be allowed to influence the sane economic policy of a state. This must be guided by objective data. As a matter of fact, the Jews constitute more than one third, thirty-five per cent, of the commercial class in Russia. If we believe our country's prosperity to be bound up with the process of its progressive industrialisation, we must admit that the part the Jews play in Russia's commercial life is tremendous, that to a considerable degree they handle her entire commerce. All that hinders the untrammelled manifestation of the Jewish economic energies is harmful to Russia's economic organism.

"If there were no Jews now in Russia, it would be necessary to invite them, in the interests of both the commercial and industrial development of the country, just as they were more than once invited for the same purposes in the past." This conclusion, reached by a student of the Jewish question in Russia, is eminently and profoundly true. The opinion of an individual student may not appear authoritative, but it has been many a time endorsed by social groups and organisations. We need not go far back into history to find facts of this sort. In 1912 at the time when the customary fair was in full swing, the Governor of Nizhni-Novgorod showed an unusual zeal in persecuting the Jews. This was in all probability connected with the Duma pre-election campaign. The "Society of the Manufacturers and Mill Owners of the Moscow Industrial Section," an organisation which is rather far from being liberal in its opinions, saw fit to interfere in its own interests. A memoir dealing with the prohibitive measures directed against the Jews was composed and presented, through the president of the Society, Mr. Goujon, to the chairman of the Council of the Ministers. Here is a quotation from this memoir: "In the economic life of the country the Jews play the part of middlemen, placed between the producer and the consumer of goods. In the Northwestern, Southern, and Southwestern provinces this function is almost exclusively that of the Jews. To isolate under such conditions, the commercial and industrial population of a considerable section of the country from the centre of its manufacturing districts is equivalent to inflicting a tremendous loss not only on the Jewish merchant class but also on the many millions of the non-Jewish population... To isolate the village from the town, the towns of the West and South from the towns and villages of the Centre and the East, is to disturb intentionally the economic life of the country, to undermine credit and depreciate the people's labour."

That is the opinion of the Moscow manufacturers. Well aware of the real needs of the country, and unwilling to sacrifice their commercial interests to anti-humanitarian mottoes, they expressed their fear that the actions of the administration would hinder the realisation of the harvest and that the "stocks of goods would find neither consumers nor buyers nor energetic middlemen to the extent to which they otherwise would have."

The Jewish people has grown to be a living part of Russia's economic organism, and the blows which are directed against the Jews affect in an equal, if not a greater, degree the mass of the aboriginal Russian population. We do not intend to discuss here the Zionistic dreams and aspirations of the Jews. One thing is clear to us, namely, that a complete exodus of the Jews from Russia would be greatly detrimental to her economic development. The Western world understands this truth very well. Werner Sombart in his work Die Zukunft der Juden (The Future of the Jews) reaches the following conclusion: "If by a miracle all the Jews would decide to-morrow to emigrate to Palestine we (the Germans) would never allow them to. For it would mean a catastrophe in the field of economic relation, not to speak of other fields, such as we have never as yet experienced and which would probably cripple our economic organism forever."

But we, Russians, give little thought to such questions. As late as the year 1914 we did not hesitate to inaugurate new restrictive measures, which it took the great trial of this War to stop.

Whoever has our economic welfare at heart, whoever dreams about the mighty development of our country and of its real emancipation from foreign influence,—inasmuch as this is generally possible,—must understand that anti-Semitism is the worst foe of our economic prosperity, that, in short, the Jewish question is a Russian question. Full rights for the Jews, equal with those that the rest of the population of the Empire enjoy, are an indispensable condition for our peaceful cultural development. Only on that basis can we achieve the broad ideals which have come into prominence in this tragic struggle with German imperialism.

The War and the Status of the Jew

By Prince Paul Dolgorukov

Prince Paul Dmitriyevich Dolgorukov, a prominent leader of the emancipatory movement in Russia, was born in 1866. He is one of the founders of the Constitutional Democratic party, and for a while he stood at the head of the Central Committee of this party. He was a member of the Second Duma, where he represented the city of Moscow.

The storm that has recently swept over our country brought to light a series of conditions which have been weighing down upon the Russian nation for a good many years. These conditions on account of their long duration have come to be considered as something habitual. The impossibility of their further continuance, at least in their present form, has suddenly become quite apparent.

The first among these is the existing attitude toward peoples whose fate is closely interwoven with the fate of Russia. The need for a new policy toward the Poles has been recognised officially and solemnly. The hour for settling the Jewish question has also struck. The contrast between the duties and responsibilities of the Jew toward the state and his position in the country where he is deprived of all rights and privileges has always existed; during the war this contradiction has become

75

so pronounced that it is impossible to overlook it any longer.

Hundreds of thousands of Jews are shedding their blood for Russia, while at home they are deprived of such elementary rights as other Russian subjects could lose only when convicted of crime. When a population of six million occupies such a position, the fact is bound to make itself felt in all walks of life; but what the war has made supremely clear is the limitations to which the Jew is subjected as to his right to choose freely his place of residence and to give his children an education.

The so-called "Pale of Settlement," Poland and the south-western section, constituted the arena for the early operations of the war. The tradesmen, the merchants, all people of any means were ruined; the poor workman was left without a crust of bread. The invading foe forced both these groups to flee. Where were they to flee? The simplest solution that presented itself was for them to go into other cities of the "Pale." But the burden of the war was felt there also. The chief breadwinner of the family had gone to war; both industries and trades were crippled. Emigration, the safety valve of poverty, was now impossible. Into the midst of this suffering came pouring in the refugees from the border regions, on the one hand, and on the other, the exiles from Germany and Austria, where they had previously found food and shelter, and whence they had now, so to speak, been thrown overboard.

The economic role of such an element, hungry and unemployed, is easily appraised. Small wonder, then, that such a condition should become absolutely unbearable; starvation has become a common occurrence, and many prefer suicide to asking for alms. And should some of these care to ask for aid there is no one who could offer it, since the local population cannot cope with the need that has so suddenly swooped down upon them.

Russia is a vast country, as is the soul of the Russian. Enough land and bread exists for all its children. Many have relatives who would welcome the refugees and exiles into their homes for the time being; many could earn their livelihood. But in accordance with the existing regulations the authorities must observe that no one who has not the right of residence should come without the "Pale." The absurdity of such regulations becomes more apparent when applied to participants in the war. Thousands of wounded Jewish soldiers are scattered all over Russia, many outside the "Pale." Their own may not come to stay with them nor even visit them. Should one of these wounded die, his people are deprived of the privilege of paying their last respects to him; unless they choose to violate the law and remain during the visit in hiding without registering their arrival.

The conditions under which the Jewish child may be educated are at present fraught with similar difficulties. A great number of educational institutions in the south and west are now closed. The parents are recommended to transfer their children to other cities—in which case the local schools have been allowed to accept Jewish pupils in excess of their regulation percentage. But the possibility of utilising this privilege in institutions outside of the "Pale" is in its turn combined with the "right of settlement," which condition certainly limits the application of this privilege. With this exception, all other educational institutions of higher and middle grades, strictly observe the usual percentage and the drawing of lots, on the basis of which the Jewish students are accepted. These limitations have become especially conspicuous, because the war has completely done away with the possibility of entering the universities of Germany and Austria, to which the Jewish youth flocked prior to the war.

Another question arises: Where should the Jewish students, who have begun their studies at a foreign university, now turn? In vain do they knock at the doors of the higher institutions; these remain closed to them, in spite of the fact that there are many vacancies there. They cannot get back to the universities of either Germany or Austria. Thus must they waste years of persistent effort and vast amounts of energy, and very many of them will not be in a position to continue their studies, and subsequently serve their own country, which is so sadly in need of educated men. Are all these discriminations against Jewish people essential for the great Russia, which is now called upon to free nations and peoples from a foreign tyranny?

The complete abrogation of all national disabilities must pass through our legislative institutions, but the loosening of the existing limitations is a measure which it is perfectly possible to take at once.

Jewish Rights and their Enemies

By Maxim Kovalevsky

Professor Maxim Maximovich Kovalevsky, one of the greatest Russian sociologists, was born in 1851. Owing to his political convictions, he had to leave Russia. In 1901 he founded in Paris the Russian Higher School of Social Sciences, the faculty of which consisted of exiled Russian scholars and political emigrants. In 1905 he came back to Russia, resumed his University work and took an active part in the political movement. In 1906 he was elected to the Duma and in 1907 to the Imperial Council. He died in 1916.

If the question should be put as to who at present stands in the way of Jewish equal rights and who demands still further limitations of the Jews' participation in both military and civil service, the answer is that no one class follows a more systematic and more definite programme in this connection than the League of United Nobility. In the year 1913 one of their conventions made the following recommendations, recorded in a volume published in the name of the league, and here quoted literally:

"I. Jews and converted Jews should not be allowed to serve in the army and navy either as regular recruits or as volunteers, nor should they be admitted to military schools.

"II. Jews and converted Jews should not be allowed to take part in the electoral conventions of the Zemstvos.

"III. Jews and converted Jews are not to be permitted to serve in the Zemstvos.

"IV. Jews and converted Jews are not to be permitted to serve in any municipal capacity.

"V. Jews and converted Jews should not be permitted to enter the civil service.

"VI. Jews and converted Jews should not be included in the lists of jurors; they may not be appointed or elected to serve in courts, they may not practice as either advocates or attorneys."

These recommendations are clearly at variance with the trend of Russian legislation throughout the reigns of Peter the Great, Catherine the Second and Alexander the First. Peter the Great called into the service of the Russian government all subjects irrespective of their nationality or religion. His fellow champions were representatives of different nationalities such as Bruce, Bauer, Repnin, Menshicov and Yaguzhinsky. As to Catherine the Second, our code of laws still retains the expression of her wish that all the peoples of Russia, each according to the precepts of its religion, should pray to the Almighty for the welfare of its rulers, and should all be equally benefited by its government.

In his "Principles of the Russian Governmental Law" Professor Gradovsky says: "In the reign of Peter the Great there were no general regulations concerning the Jews." Measures against the Jews date from the reign of Catherine the First. During the reign of Catherine the Second, little was added to the existing array of limitations. In the districts in which the first Partition of Poland found them, the Jews at that time enjoyed almost all the rights of the native Russian citizen. Although the Empress recognized the "Pale of Settlement" created in the reign of Peter the Second, she, nevertheless, stretched its boundaries to include not only Little Russia but also the Vice-Royalty of Ekaterinoslav and the province of Taurida, wherein the Jews were granted all rights of citizenship. In the "Regulations Concerning the Jews" published in 1804, in the reign of Alexander the First, the principle of equal civil rights for this nation is brought out in Article 42. "All the Jews in Russia," says this article, "whether residents or new settlers or foreigners coming to transact business are free and are to be under the protection of the law on a par with other Russian subjects." In commenting upon this article, Professor Gradovsky writes that this is clearly an attempt to fuse the Jewish nation with the rest of the Russian population by giving the former definite civil rights.

Only during the last year of the reign of Alexander the First were some measures adopted whereby the "Pale of Settlement" was narrowed down because of a certain sect of "Sabbathists," closely related to Judaism, which had greatly increased in numbers, particularly in the provinces of Voronezh, Samara, Tula, and others. According to the "Regulations Concerning the Jews" of 1835, enacted in the reign of Nicholas the First, the Jews retained the right to own all kinds of real estate, with the exception of inhabited estates and to deal in all kinds of merchandise on the same basis as the other citizens,—of course, only within the "Pale."

It is noteworthy that at this time the Jews were allowed to attend governmental schools of all grades, and that graduates from these were granted certain privileges. It is only toward the end of the reign of Nicholas I that the government adopts a system of limitations relating to the Jews, without, however, restraining their right to attend the governmental educational institutions. On the 31st of March, 1856, an imperial edict was issued ordering a revision of the existing regulations relating to the Jews. Therein it is clearly stated that the purpose of this revision is to conciliate these regulations with the intention of the government to fuse this people with the native population of the land. During the entire reign of Alexander II no limitations existed for the entrance of Jews into the Universities and the other educational institutions. On the contrary, according to Gradovsky, the limitations within the "Pale" did not apply to persons desiring to obtain a higher education, namely to those entering the medical academy, the universities, and the Institute of Technology. Gradovsky refers to the continuation of the "Code of Laws," of 1868. The book was published in 1875, while this freedom was in full swing. Within the "Pale," the Jews had equal commercial rights with other citizens. Until the Polish rebellion of 1863 the Jews were permitted to own real estate, not only in cities but also in rural districts. After the rebellion this was forbidden to them as well as to the Poles. The foreign Jew could come to Russia freely and register on the same foreign passport as would be required from any other citizen of that country.

From what has been said, it follows that many of the limitations, which at present weigh down upon the Jews have been created only recently. The present reign, too, was begun with measures favoring the Jew. In 1903, in spite of the fact that the Jews, in accordance with a law which was confirmed in 1872, were forbidden to live in villages even within the "Pale," two hundred of these villages were turned into towns, and later fifty-seven more were added to this number. The measure rendered these places legally habitable by the Jews. On August 11, 1904, a law was passed wherein it was emphatically stated that Jews who were graduates from a university were to be permitted to live freely everywhere in the Empire. But since the repression of the revolutionary movement, this privilege has become a pretext for the restriction of the admittance of Jews into higher educational institutions.

From the viewpoint of the interests of the Russian state, the existing disabilities of the Jews are detrimental both to our economic life, and to the mutual relations among our citizens; they also work havoc upon the progress of education as well as upon the raising of the general level of our culture. Measures limiting a portion of the population in its rights to acquire property, to obtain an education in middle and higher state schools, to assume the responsibilities of a judge or of a lawyer, and, in general, restraining its freedom to pursue a professional career—are clearly irreconcilable with the promises given us in the manifesto of the 17th of October, 1906.

The fear that the granting of equal rights to the Jews may deprive the peasant of his land, is perfectly groundless. There are many other means whereby the tiller of the soil may be assured the possession of a portion of land. In the West we have systems such as that of the homestead, based on the inalienability of the family property (bien de famille). Such systems may be traced back as far as the Middle Ages. The medieval law forbids the taking away from the peasant, even for arrearage, of his agricultural implements and the cattle necessary for his labour,—not to speak of his land, which, however, it would be impossible to take away, since it is the suzerain that is its rightful owner. The indivisibility of the family estate, which only a short time ago was recognised by the Appellatory Division of our Senate, with reference to the Western Section, was achieving the same results because for the sale of such property the agreement of all the members of the family was required. Such a protection of the interests of the peasant landowner is essential in his relation to the capitalist, whether it be a member of the landed gentry or a wealthy peasant, known as a Kulak, or a Jew who lends money at interest, or an Armenian or, for that matter, a usurer of the Orthodox faith. In order that the land be retained by the peasant it is far more essential that only members of the peasant class be allowed to attend the auction sales of land sold because of the owner's arrears. And yet our law has permitted outsiders to attend if not the first auction sale, at least the second. I am strongly in favour of protecting the peasant's property, but I cannot see that to achieve this goal, it is necessary for a body politic based on law to limit any one's freedom of moving about, settling or choosing a profession. This view is shared by some of the political writers in Russia who, like the late B.N. Chicherin, Professor of the University of Moscow, have identified their names with the defence of the idea of equal rights for the Jews.

Jewish Market in Moscow, c.1903.
Library of Congress Prints and Photographs Division
Washington, D.C. 20540 USA

The Jewish Question as a Russian Question

By Dmitry Merezhkovsky

Dmitry Sergeyevich Merezhkovsky occupies an important place in modern Russian letters and religious philosophy. He is responsible for several books of poems and for a series of ponderous historical novels. He is also the author of numerous critical studies distinguished by an original method and an extraordinary brilliancy. He was born in 1866.

Russia ... Russia alone should be our deepest concern at present. The destiny of the numerous races and nationalities that go to make Russia is the destiny of the Russian Empire itself. One would ascertain the attitude of these nationalities by asking them: "Are you with Russia or is it your desire to exist apart from her? If you desire to exist apart from her—why, then, do you appeal to us for help? If with us—let us then, in this time of terror, disdain to consider our personal fortunes and let our thoughts be with Russia and with her alone. For without her your existence is inconceivable; her rise is your rise and her fall is your fall."

We would like very much to say that there is no such thing as the Jewish, Polish, Ukrainian, Armenian, Georgian, question, that there is only one question—

the Russian. Yes, we would like to, but we cannot; the Russian people have yet to earn the right to say that, and therein lies their tragedy.... The moment Russian idealism ventures to tackle any of those complicated national home problems,—it becomes weak, impotent and therefore irresponsible.

The Jewish question is a striking illustration of what we have just said. What do we owe the Jews? Indignation? Or the admission that anti-Semitism is abominable? But we admitted that a long time ago, and our indignation runs so high and is so clearly outspoken that it is beyond one's power even to speak calmly of it. The only thing we can do is to join our voice to that of the Jews. And we do.

But outcries, loud as they may be, are not sufficient, and it is the consciousness of the fact, that the outcries are insufficient and that at the present moment we possess no other weapons with which to fight the evil that wearies and harrows us.

What misery, and pain, and shame!

But in spite of the pain and the shame we cry out and reiterate and declare to the people around us, who are ignorant of the table of multiplication, that two and two make four, that the Jews are human beings like us; that they are neither enemies nor traitors to their country; that they are as good citizens as we are; that they love Russia no less than we do, and that anti-Semitism is a disgraceful stigma upon Russia's face. But apart from our righteous indignation, may we not be allowed calmly to utter one thought that occurs to us at this moment?

"Judophilism" and "Judophobia" are closely related. A blind denial of a nationality engenders an equally blind affirmation of it. An absolute "Nay" naturally brings forth an absolute "Yea."

Whom do we call a "Judophile" in Russia at the present time? Presumably, it is he or she who loves the Jews with a singular love, who finds in them greater values than in any other nationality. In the eyes of the so-called "true Russians" we, the Intellectuals, are such Judophiles.

"Why worry over the Jews all the time?" the Russian Nationalists say to us. Now, how on earth can we stop worrying over the Jews, and, for that matter, over the Poles, Armenians, Ukrainians, Georgians, and so forth? When in our presence some one is being outraged, we cannot merely pass on; it is not humane. We must help him who is being assailed. At least, we ought to join our voice with his in crying out for help. This is precisely what we have been doing, and woe to us, if we cease to do it, cease to be human beings in order to become Russians.

A forest of national problems has grown around us, and the sounds of the Russian language are being drowned by the voices of all the numerous peoples that inhabit Russia. It is inevitable and just. We are not well, but with them it is still worse. We have great pain, but their's is greater. We must forget ourselves for their sake.

That is why we say to the "Nationalists":

Cease oppressing the non-Russian element of our empire, so that we may have the right to be Russians, and that we may with dignity show our national face, as that of a human being, not that of a beast. Cease to be 'Judophobes' so that we may cease to be 'Judophiles.' Here is an instance taken at random.

The Jewish question has a religious as well as a national aspect. Between Judaism and Christianity, as between two poles, there are strong attractions and equally strong repulsions. Judaism gave birth to Christianity. The New Testament issued from the Old Testament. Paul the Apostle, who more than any one else fought Judaism, wrote: "For I could wish that myself were accursed from Christ for my brethren, my kinsmen according to the flesh."

But whereas we may speak of attractions, it is not well for us to speak of repulsions. Indeed, how can we quarrel with him, who has no voice? The disabilities of the Jews seal our lips. We must not separate Christianity from Judaism, for it means, as one Jew put it, the establishment of another, spiritual "Pale of Settlement." Let us do away with the physical Pale, then we will be able to discuss the spiritual one. Until then, all our protestations and declarations of righteousness will only prove to the Jews our insincerity.

Why has the Jewish question become so keen in time of war? For the same reason that the rest of the national problems have made themselves felt.

We have called the present struggle a war of liberation. We entered the war with the avowed purpose of liberating those who are situated at a distance from us. While liberating distant strangers, why then do we oppress those who live close by our side? We wage war against tyranny outside of Russia, and we allow oppression to reign within her. We pity everybody but the Jews. Why?

Are they not dying on the battlefields for our sake? Do they not love us—who hate them? Do we not hate them—who love us? If we continue to act as we have done in the past, would not everybody lose faith in us, and would not the nations of the earth be justified in saying to us: "You can love only from afar. You are liars!"

We believed our righteousness to be our strongest weapon. We wanted to conquer brute force by the truth. If we persist in this desire, let us not lie; let us not weaken our truth by falsehood.

The Teutons say: "We fight to be the rulers of the world,"—and they act accordingly. We say: "We fight for universal peace, for the emancipation of the world," but we do not act accordingly.

Let us begin then with the liberation of the Jews at home. Let the oppressed nations in our land bear in mind, however, that only a free Russian people will be able to give them freedom.

Let the Jews remember that the Jewish question is a Russian question.

Papershop in Jewish ghetto, Vilna, Russia (1922).
Frank Carpenter Collection.
Library of Congress Prints and Photographs Division
Washington, D.C. 20540 USA

Concerning the Ideology of the Jewish Question

By Vyacheslav Ivanov

Vyacheslav Ivanovich Ivanov was born in 1866. A poet of great mastery and a refined critic, his thought, is steeped in Hellenism and in the most abstruse mystic lore.

One of the wiliest and the most harmful doctrines of our times is, I believe, the fashionable ideology of spiritual anti-Semitism. It attributes to Aryanism, which by the way, is a quantity ethnically if not linguistically enigmatical, many excellent and splendid qualities, while in the Semitic influences and admixtures to the Aryan element it sees nothing but negative energies, which have always hindered the free unfolding of the creative powers of the Aryan genius.

This doctrine would deprive Hellenism of Aphrodite, who came to the Hellenes from the Semites, and would cut the main and most profound root of Christianity, namely its faith in a "transcendental," or, plainly, living God. Spiritual anti-Semitism cuts the body of Christianity into two halves, and keeps only that half whose forms are justified by analogies borrowed from the Greek religious thought, justified, in the eyes of learned dodgers who choose to play the part of Romanticists of Aryanism.

This anti-religious and secretly anti-Christian theory, one of the Trojan wooden horses made in Germany, was clearly intended to "Indo-Germanize" the world, when suddenly the twilight of the Gods swooped down upon the Berlin Valhalla. Nevertheless it has succeeded in seducing many minds, obscured by prejudices. It was hailed by "immanent" philosophers and anti-Semites out of political considerations and psychological pre-dispositions, as well as by Christians mindless of their kin, by anti-church people of all kinds, and even by atheists of Jewish birth, who are ashamed of their kin and who are in the world like salt which has lost its strength.

The more vivid and profound the church conscious-ness is in a Christian, the more vividly and profoundly does he feel himself, I shall not say a philo-Semite, but truly a Semite in spirit. We have so thoroughly con-fused, distorted and forgotten all the holy and true tra-ditions, we have so thoroughly lost the habit of applying our reason to the lucid, old truths learned by heart, that this statement may sound like a paradox.

Vladimir Solovyov's touching affection for Judaism is a plain and natural manifestation of his love for Christ and of his inner experience of being merged in the Church. The body of the Church is for the mystic the true, although invisible body of Christ, and through Christ it is the body begotten of Abraham's seed. The latter body, like the curtain of the temple in Jerusalem in the hour of our Saviour's death, was rent in twain, and that half of it which is Judaism passionately seeks the whole, longs and yearns, and pours out its wrath

94

upon the second half, which in its turn longs for the reunion and the integrity of mystic Israel.

Whoever is within the Church loves Mary; and whoever loves Mary loves also Israel whose name together with those of the patriarchs and prophets solemnly resounds in our liturgical hymns. The minds of those who in various times represented the earthly organisation of the Church could be poisoned by hatred of the Jews, in whom they suspected Christ's enemies, precisely because it seemed to them that the Jewish nation was already void of the true Jewish spirit and was not of Abraham's seed. But what do all these errings mean in face of the single testimony of the apostle Paul?

I have placed myself, in these lines, on the standpoint of religious thought, and I wish to remind people of the truth that to be a Christian means to be not a heathen, not simply an Aryan by blood, but to become through baptism, which sacramentally includes also circumcision, a child of Abraham, and, therefore, in a sacramental sense a brother to Abraham's descendants, who, according to the word of the apostle, are not deprived of inheritance, and whom, according to Christ's word, we must bless even if they curse us. Personally, I do not believe that the Jews hate Christ, unless it be that they hate Him in spite of their secret, presensuous love for Him, hate Him with that peculiar hatred which comes from jealousy and which the Hellenes defined as the negative hypostase of Eros, as anti-Eros.

I think that Providence has appointed the Jews eternally to test the Christian peoples in their love for Christ and in their faithfulness to Him. And when His work will be consummated in us, then their demands and expectations will be fulfilled and they will be convinced that they need not wait for another Messiah. As for us, if we were walking with Christ, we would not fear our examiners: for love conquers fear.

The accounts the Russian soul has to settle with that of the Jew are complex. In spite of the fact they have frequently and most completely been united in suffering, the Jew is loath to love that which is most sacred to the Russian soul. For the benefit of those in whom resound the separate clashing voices of this spiritual dispute, I shall quote in conclusion this final and irrevocable verdict of Dostoyevsky, who had the reputation of being an anti-Semite: "All that is demanded by humanity, justice and Christian law, must be done for the Jews. I shall add to these words that in spite of the considerations exposed above, I definitely stand for an increase of the Jewish rights in formal legislation and, if possible, for the removal of all the legal disabilities which stand in the way of their equality with the rest of the population (although in some cases they have already more rights than the aboriginal population, or, better, they have greater possibilities to utilise the rights which they enjoy)." ("A Writer's Journal," March, 1877, III, p. 4.)

The Little Boy

By Maxim Gorky

I t is hard to tell this little story,—it is so simple. When I was a youth, I used to gather the children of our street on Sunday mornings during the spring and summer seasons and take them with me to the fields and woods. I took great pleasure in the friendship of these little people, who were as gay as birds.

The children were only too glad to leave the dusty, narrow streets of the city. Their mothers provided them with slices of bread, while I bought them dainties and filled a big bottle with cider, and like a shepherd, walked behind my carefree little lambs, while we passed through the town and the fields on our way to the green forest, beautiful and caressing in its array of Spring.

We always started on our journey early in the morning when the church bells were ushering in the early mass, and we were accompanied by the chimes and the clouds of dust raised by the children's nimble feet.

In the heat of noon, exhausted with playing, my companions would gather at the edge of the forest, and after that, having eaten their food, the smaller children would lie down and sleep in the shade of hazel and snow-ball trees, while the ten-year-old boys would flock around me and ask me to tell them stories. I would satisfy their desire, chattering as eagerly as the children themselves, and often, in spite of the self-assurance of youth and the ridiculous pride which it takes in the miserable crumbs of worldly wisdom it possesses, I would feel like a twenty-year-old child in a conclave of sages.

Overhead is the blue veil of the spring sky, and before us lies the deep forest, brooding in wise silence. Now and then the wind whispers gently and stirs the fragrant shadows of the forest, and again does the soothing silence caress us with a motherly caress. White clouds are sailing slowly across the azure heavens. Viewed from the earth, heated by the sun, the sky appears cold, and it is strange to see the clouds melt away in the blue. And all around me—little people, dear little people, destined to partake of all the sorrows and all the joys of life.

These were my happy days, my true holidays, and my soul already dusty with the knowledge of life's evil was bathed and refreshed in the clear-eyed wisdom of child-like thoughts and feelings.

Once, when I was coming out of the city on my way to the fields, accompanied by a crowd of children we met an unknown little Jewish boy. He was barefooted and his shirt was torn; his eyebrows were black, his body slim and his hair grew in curls like that of a little sheep. He was excited and he seemed to have been crying. The lids of his dull-black eyes, swollen and red, contrasted with his face, which, emaciated by starvation, was ghastly pale.

Having found himself face to face with the crowd of children, he stood still in the middle of the road, burrowing his bare feet in the dust, which early in the morning is so deliciously cool. In fear, he half opened the dark lips of his fair mouth,—the next second he leaped right on to the sidewalk.

"Catch him!" the children started to shout gaily and in a chorus. "A Jewish boy! Catch the Jew boy!"

I waited, thinking that he would run away. His thin, big-eyed face was all fear; his lips quivered; he stood there amid the shouts and the mocking laughter. Pressing his shoulders against the fence and hiding his hands behind his back, he stretched and strangely appeared to have grown bigger.

But suddenly he spoke,—very calmly and in a distinct and correct Russian.

"If you wish,—I will show you some tricks."

I took this offer for a means of self-defence. But the children at once became interested. The larger and coarser boys alone looked with distrust and suspicion on the little Jewish boy. The children of our street were in a state of guerrilla warfare with the children of other streets; in addition, they were deeply convinced of their own superiority and were loath to brook the rivalry of other children.

The smaller boys approached the matter more simply. "Come on, show us," they shouted.

The handsome, slim boy moved away from the fence, bent his thin body backward, and touching the ground with his hands, he tossed up his feet and remained standing on his arms, shouting: "Hop! Hop! Hop!"

Then he began to spin in the air, swinging his body lightly and adroitly. Through the holes of his shirt and pants we caught glimpses of the greyish skin of his slim body, of his sharply bulging and angular shoulder-blades, knees and elbows. It seemed to us as if with one more twist of his body his thin bones would crack and break into pieces.

He worked hard until the shirt grew wet with sweat about his shoulders. After each especially daring feat he looked into the children's faces with an artificial, weary smile, and it was unpleasant to see his dull eyes, grown large with pain. Their strange and unsteady glance was not like that of a child.

The lads encouraged him with loud outcries. Many imitated him, rolling in the dust and shouting for joy, pain and envy. But the joyous minutes were soon over when the boy, bringing his exhibition to an end, looked upon the children with the benevolent smile of a thoroughbred artist and stretching forth his hand said: "Now give me something."

We all became silent, until one of the children said: "Money?"

"Yes," said the lad.

"Look at him," said the children. "For money, we could do those tricks ourselves."

The audience became hostile toward the artist, and betook itself to the field, ridiculing and insulting him. Of course, none of them had any money. I myself, had only seven kopecks about me. I put two coins in the boy's dusty palm. He moved them with his finger and with a kindly smile said: "Thank you."

He went away, and I noticed that his shirt around his back was all in black blotches and was clinging close to his shoulder-blades.

"Hold on, what is it?"

He stopped, turned about, scrutinised me and said distinctly, with the same kindly smile: "You mean the blotches on my back? That's from falling off the trapeze.

It happened on Easter. My father is still lying in bed, but I am quite well now."

I lifted his shirt. On his back, running down from his left shoulder to the side, was a wide dark scratch which had now become dried up into a thick crust. While he was exhibiting his tricks the wound broke open in several spots and red blood was now trickling from the openings.

"It doesn't hurt any more," said he with a smile. "It doesn't hurt, it only itches."

And bravely, as it becomes a hero, he looked in my eyes and went on, speaking like a serious grown-up person: "You think—I have been doing this for myself? Upon my word—I have not. My father ... there is not a crust of bread in the house, and my father is lying badly hurt. So you see, I have to work hard. And to make matters worse, we are Jews, and everybody laughs at us. Good-bye."

He spoke with a smile, cheerfully and courageously. With a nod of his curly head, he quickly went on, passing by the houses which looked at him with their glass eyes, indifferent and dead.

All this is insignificant and simple, is it not? Yet many a time in the darkest days of my life I remembered with gratitude the courage and bravery of the little Jewish boy. And now, in these sorrowful days of suffering and bloody outrages which fall upon the grey head of the ancient nation, the creator of Gods and religion,—I think again of the boy, for in him I see the symbol of true manly bravery,—not the pliant patience of slaves, who live by uncertain hopes, but the courage of the strong who are certain of their victory.

Jewish children in a street of Warsaw, Poland, Russia.
Photographed and published by B.W. Kilburn, c. 1897.
Library of Congress Prints and Photographs Division
Washington, D.C. 20540 USA

The Fatherland for All

By Fyodor Sologub

Fyodor Sologub is the pseudonym of Fyodor
Kuzmich Teternikov, novelist and poet. A considerable portion of his prose works has been recently
made accessible to the English reader. Sologub's
poetic output includes lyrical pieces of rare beauty.
He was born in 1864.

The great war, which we did not want, but which
we are conducting with intense fervour, exert-
ing all our spiritual and material forces, has put
before our consciousness and our moral sense the fundamental problems of our social and political organisation. Not in vain have the newspapers hastened to
style this war a Fatherland War. The question of the
Fatherland has suddenly acquired for us a peculiar
keenness and significance.

The war has taken Russian society and the Russian
people by surprise, but luckily it has come to us at the
moment when the questions which were confronting
us had already been settled both in our reason and
conscience. The heroic labour of the Russian intellectual has not been in vain. And now what we have to do
is not to argue and demonstrate, but to determine the
meaning of events. And the meaning of what is going
on is such that we are forced to consider this war not
only as one of defence, but also as one of emancipa-

tion. It appears to us not only as a struggle for the rights of small states threatened by large ones, and as a war against German militarism, but also as a strife against...[1] internal danger, whatever may be the various forms this danger assumes.

The first and chief danger which threatened, and is still threatening us, is the danger of internal division and disorder. The equal readiness and zeal to stand up for her which all the peoples inhabiting Russia have manifested has shown how unjust is the preaching of hatred and of narrow nationalism. The peoples who bear the same burdens of our state as the Russians do, who defend our common fatherland just as faithfully as the Russians, thereby assert that our fatherland is for all, that Russia is for every one who is considered a Russian subject and meets his duties toward the state. Russia is not only for those who are Russians by language and birth, she is for all who live under her sovereign dominion. No one in Russia is benefited by the unequal rights of her various peoples; this inequality does not add to our political power, it only supports our internal disorder. Its abolition by no means contradicts the fundamental conceptions of Russian statehood.

You will say that Russia has been created by the Russian race. Well, then, her policy must be determined by the qualities of the Russian popular spirit,—but animosity and exclusiveness are things strange and repulsive to it. The soul of the Russian people is trusting and open to all influences. And this is only natural: only that nation can become the basis of a great state which is able with ease and joy to unite with all the races it meets on its historic road. The history of Russia illus-

104

trates this. Besides, who has ever asserted that people born unto the Russian tongue are racially pure Slavs?

You will say that Russia is a Christian state. Agreed. But do not Christ's commandments teach us to see a friend and a brother and one's equal in every man? The more we are Christians, the less of animosity and exclusiveness can be in our hearts. What difference does it make that two men speak different languages and pray in different ways? When it is a question of paying duties and taxes, and bearing arms in defence of the fatherland, religious and race peculiarities do not matter.

The fatherland is for all of us, because we are all for the fatherland. The fatherland is our common home, and this home we build, keep in good order, and defend. We build our common home not like hirelings, to whom, after they get their pay, the building becomes alien. In rearing, decorating and defending it we bargain with no one, we give everything that is necessary for its upbuilding and defence,—we give our property, our labour, our very life. Even when our labour appears selfish, even then—provided it is not criminal—it is for the good of our common home: for, all that adds to the happiness, well-being and freedom of each one living in the home, adds to its strength and beauty.

We build our common home, decorate it and defend it, and we do it with joy and willingness because in our common home we are neither hirelings nor guests. In our common home, then, who are we? We must know and always remember that in our common home we are all masters of the house. It is not our right, but our duty toward our home, of which we must take care just as every good master takes care of his house. The consciousness of the fact that we are the masters of our common home is clear; for it is seen that every one of us in whom conscience and reason do not slumber, feels responsible for the disorder of our life.

Not an outsider, nor a congress of allies, nor some one social class shall regulate our affairs for the best of Poland, Finland, the Jews and the rest. Neither our allies, nor any one of our social classes, nor the wisest and strongest among us,—but all of us Russian citizens, all of us who joyously and willingly bear the burden of statehood, are called upon to settle in conscience and reason, the fundamental problems of our great home-building.

In the face of the common foe we are all united. We have mustered all our forces for the defence of our native land from the hostile invasion. We are all brothers, all children of one fatherland, and to all Russia is a good mother loving all equally well. Many are the peoples Russia has gathered under her dominion and she is to all equally benevolent.

How eager is one to say these words, to have the right to utter them! But we have it not. Not toward all is Russia equally benevolent, and in the hour of great trials and high deeds she is still unable, still unwilling, to tear asunder the fatal chain, the terrible "Pale of Settlement."

Whenever I met Russian Jews abroad, I always marvelled at the strangely tenacious love for Russia which they preserve. They speak of Russia with the same longing and the same tenderness as the Russian emigrants; they are equally eager to return and equally saddened if the return is impossible. Wherefore should they love Russia, who is so harsh and inhospitable toward them?

Strange as it may sound, there are children who love their cruel stepmothers. Of course, they are exceptions; usually such stepmothers are hated. But in the case of Jews such exceptions become the general rule: the Jews love the same Russia that is so cruel toward them.

Some one's interests demand that the Jews should be oppressed, stabled in the "Pale of Settlement," limited in the right to education, and in other respects. But to whose interest is it? Russia's? Surely not.

Social relations in Russia, as in every civilised state, must rest on the immovable foundations of justice, reason, and conscience. All those persons who are united by the fact of their belonging to the Russian state must have, within the limits of the empire, the minimum of rights, which, to our shame, are refused the Jews. This minimum each one of us receives not for his personal or racial deserts or distinctive traits, but as a citizen of the state. To obey the common Russian laws, to pay the established taxes, to serve in the army,—all these are the duties of a Russian subject, corresponding to the amount of rights of which he can be deprived only by a court ruling for a crime.

A man not dishonoured by a court decision may not live where he wants to,—because he is a Jew; a boy who has not been dismissed from any school for deficiency or misconduct, may not enter the "gymnasium," where there are plenty of vacancies, but where the few vacancies set aside by a percentage rule for the Jewish brats, are eagerly filled by them; a soldier's wife may not visit her wounded and agonising husband because he happens to be dying outside the "Pale"; the deceased may not be buried in the town where he died, for he had no right of residence in that town,—what does all this mean? Who needs all this?

All these people are Russian subjects, not our enemies, and yet they are treated in this fashion. What is the purpose of it all? Is it in order to kindle among the Jews the fire of implacable hatred of Russia and turn them into our enemies? But then we must be logical and not tolerate them in the "Pale of Settlement"; we must exile or destroy them. But a civilised state will never persuade itself to commit such acts, inhuman though logical. And if it does not decide to do that, it must, for the sake of its safety and dignity, grant to every Russian citizen the elementary human rights. It is imperative that every Russian citizen should have every reason to love Russia and no right to hate her. If that portion of the Russian population which is deprived of rights still loves Russia, it is because the people of purely Russian extraction have no hatred for people of non-Russian birth, and our co-citizens are fully aware of it. They know that their disabilities are a burden to ourselves.

The removal of the Jewish disabilities is most imperatively dictated to us also by our dignity as a body politic. The name of Russian subject must be respected within our country, for otherwise the civilised world will not grow accustomed to respect Russia. Our country is feared for its military might and loved for the fine qualities of its people, but it will be respected only when it becomes a land of free men.

Footnotes:
[1] Several words here are crossed out by Russian censorship.—Translator's Note.

On Nationalism

A speech delivered by Vladimir Solovyov at
a University Dinner on February 8th, 1890

Vladimir Sergeyevich Solovyov is known to the
world as the noblest and the most profound of
Russian thinkers. The author of a large number of
philosophical and theological treatises, he is also
responsible for a slender volume of exquisite poems
and a series of publicistic works, wherein the cause
of progress is vigorously upheld. Solovyov was born
in 1853 and died in 1900.

The dominating idea of the present time is the national idea. Of course, there is nothing bad about this. But the national idea as well as any other, can be very differently interpreted. The conception of nationalism which is very popular in our country reminds one of the famous answer made by a Hottentot to a missionary, who asked him whether he knows the difference between good and bad. "Sure I know," retorted the Hottentot. "Good—is when I steal other people's cattle and wives, and bad—when my own are stolen." In a like manner, many of our nationalists praise the love for their people and brand other people's patriotism as treason.

In spite of the wide diffusion of this view, I persist in my belief that the Russian national idea cannot be based on a Hottentot-like morality, that it cannot exclude the principles of justice and all-human solidarity. It is time that we should see the realisation of the true Russian idea and of all that it implies, namely: Poland's autonomy, Jewish equal rights and the untrammelled development of all the nationalities that people the Russian Empire.

Concerning the Legal Status of the Jews

By Count Ivan Tolstoy

Count Ivan Ivanovich Tolstoy, born in 1858, occupied the post of Minister of Public Instruction at the time of Count Witte's premiership. In 1907 he was a candidate for election to the Duma, as deputy from Petrograd. A distinguished archaeologist and connoisseur of art, he was for many years the vice-president of the Imperial Academy of Fine Arts.

"Therefore all things whatsoever ye would that men should do to you, do ye even so to them." (St. Matthew, 7, 12.) This is the divine law, which it is the task of every one who considers and feels himself a Christian to follow, and which should also be strictly observed by a State. Now, would any one of the Christians who owe their allegiance to the Russian state consent to be treated as the Jews are in Russia? Would he like to be confined within a certain definite zone of settlement, to be kept from giving his children an education, and to find himself excluded from many fields of honest and honourable endeavour? Would he like, all through his life to be humiliated before his co-citizens of other faith and birth?

You despise them, hate them, and accuse them of all that it may please any maniac or liar to invent about them. Yet you demand of the Jews that they should help you, when you stand in need of help. You, Jew-haters, serve somebody or something, but truly it is not God, it is not the cause of goodness that you are serving. In your blindness you harm, above all, yourself and our country, our dear, long-suffering Russia, whom the Jews, your co-citizens, love and cannot help loving more than you do. They know that Russia hates none of her faithful and loving children and that they are hated only by people, who, either by nature or because of a poor education, cannot exist without hating some one or something. By their deeds ye shall know them, these wolves disguised as sheep.

Combat evil and side with good, do good, and do not judge a man by the fact that his parents are Jewish or Christian, or that he was born into one faith or another. Remember that we are all born equally naked and that we must all die. Therefore, do not boast of your birth; bear firmly in mind that we are all equal before God, before Truth and that we must be equal before the Law.

As for the legal disabilities of a portion of citizens who are guilty of no crime,—such as injustice must be completely condemned. In practice, such a policy has always borne and always will bear fruits of evil. The very existence of such an injustice corrupts and puts in jeopardy the social body which tolerates it.... No benefits which may be derived by individual persons or social classes from an inequality of rights can justify the State in depriving a group of citizens of their full rights, as a result of their race and faith. This is the

A-B-C of justice, and those who do not know it have yet to learn what justice is.

Neither are the Jews better than we are, nor are we better than they. We are all human beings and, as such, we must all be equal before the impartial and dispassionate Law, which determines our rights and duties towards the State and society. Good and bad people, I repeat, are everywhere, and the proportion is roughly the same among us as among them. Let us, therefore, strive for the realisation of justice on earth, and let us believe in the final triumph of truth. The rest will be added unto us. Without such a faith it is hard to live...

Portrait of Leonid Andreyev by Ilya Repin, 1904.
Oil on canvas. 75 × 66.5 cm.
The State Tretyakov Gallery, Moscow, Russia.

The Wounded Soldier

By Leonid Andreyev

A sad and disquieting image often rises before my eyes.

It happened in Petrograd, on the staircase of a large, new building, one apartment of which was transformed into a private ward. When I entered the porter's lodge, on my way to a friend, I saw that it was filled with wounded soldiers, who had just arrived, while curious spectators crowded near the plate-glass door. The house was new and luxuriously furnished, and the elevator on which the wounded soldiers were taken up, was carefully covered with some kind of cloth, for fear that the velvet would be soiled and the insects would get into the seams. Upstairs the wounded were cordially greeted by a priest and a man dressed in white. After having kissed the priest's hand, the wounded, evidently embarrassed by the bright light and the luxury of the place, entered the ward awk-wardly and silently. There were no seriously wounded on stretchers among them, all were able to walk; yet it was painful to look at them.

There was a wounded soldier in one of the last groups taken up by the elevator who strangely attracted every-body's attention. He was a short, young, lean, ghastly pale Jew. All the wounded were pale, but there was something sinister about the pallor of his face; it was a paleness of an utterly exhausted, anaemic or fatally sick man. He was walking alone, feebly moving his feet, and like everybody else bent to kiss the hand of the priest, but he hardly knew what he was doing, and his kiss was strangely indifferent and meaningless. He was evidently wounded in his arm, which he held stretched out. Several fingers were wrapped up, the others, which were not injured, were covered with a crust of dirt and blood. But on his coat, on the back, there was a large brown blotch of blood, a very large one, covering almost half of his back and in the midst of the soft cloth it bulged stiffly as if starched. And this horrible spot told the simple story of the battle and the wound. But it was not the stain that made him so peculiarly conspicuous—other soldiers had similar blotches—it was rather his unusual pallor, thinness and smallness, and, above all, an expression of peculiar timidity, as if he was not at all sure whether his behaviour was appropriate and whether he had come to the right place. The faces of the other wounded soldiers, non-Jews, expressed nothing of the kind. These men were confused, but not afraid, and walked straight ahead, into the ward.

And then I recollected how a military sanitarian, whose duty it is to escort a train of wounded soldiers, had told me that the wounded Jews actually try not to moan. It was hardly credible, and at first I did not believe it; how was it possible, that a wounded soldier, freshly picked up from the battlefield and lying among wounded soldiers should try not to moan, as all do? But the sanitarian confirmed his statement and added: they are afraid to attract attention to themselves.

The Jewish soldier entered the ward after the others, and the door was closed, but his image, sorrowful and disquieting, lingered before my eyes. Of course, he, too, tried not to attract attention—and therein is the cause of his shyness; and when his wound will be dressed and he will be put into bed, he will also try not to moan. For, what right has he to moan aloud?

It is very possible, that he has no right of settlement in Petrograd and is allowed to stay there only as one of the wounded; a rather precarious right! And that which is home for others is nothing but a kind of honourable imprisonment for him; he will be kept for a while, then they will let him go, saying: "Go away, you must not be here."

And what if his mother, or sister, or father, who also have no right of settlement, will desire to come to him and kiss his bloodstained hand which has defended Russia—vague, distant Russia? But these reflections and questions came to my mind later. At the moment, I beheld, with the eyes of a peaceful citizen, the bloody, hardened blotch and the dreadful pallor of war, and the needless terror before that which, after all, is your own, and I felt an overwhelming depression and sadness.

Jewish girls in Samarkand.
Sergey Prokudin-Gorskii Collection (between 1905 and 1915).
Library of Congress, Washington, D.C. 20540 USA

How to Help?

By Catherine Kuskova

Catherine Kuskova is a journalist and social worker of considerable note.

Lord, what a familiar sight! How many times have we seen it during the last nine or ten months.... And every time you blush with shame and you have the feeling of being overcome and petrified in the face of the incomprehensible, elemental catastrophe.

The train slowly pulls up to the high structure of the station. The scene is laid in one of the towns of the Western section. Faces of passengers, restless, way-worn, sickly, are seen in the windows. The cars are over-crowded beyond all measure. There are many black-eyed children, with curly black locks, and also old people, decrepit with age. The railway platform is crowded with Jewish youths, with representatives of the Jewish community, and a mass of curious people who eagerly scan the newcomers. A large crowd of passengers emerge from the cars rapidly and in disorder. They are Jews deported from the zone of military operations. The local Jewish community had been notified by a telegram and now they are meeting the newcomers.

The community has seen to it that hot tea, bread, and milk for the children is served to the deported right at the station. A most timely measure! Many of them had no time even to take food along; they were deported on short notice, and, besides, a family is allowed to carry no more than forty pounds of luggage. What is forty pounds for a family often very large? They can hardly afford to take some underwear and warm clothes.... Behind each family there remained a home, probably a store, a stand, a workshop or simply a sewing-machine, the sole source of income.... All are equal now in this dreadful train, which carries them away from home, naked wrecks of humanity, torn from their customary course of life and deprived of the daily toil, which fed the family. And what a terror it is to look into their eyes. It is plainly written in them: "This is nothing, the worst is still to come."

They sat down on the benches in the waiting room, and started drinking tea, and eating. "Well, you are feeding your spies, eh?" suddenly remarks a porter, addressing a representative of the Jewish community. The latter grows pale, shivers, and quickly moves away. What, indeed, could one answer? How does this great migration of a people impress an unsophisticated brain? If the entire population leaves a district the matter is clear; the place must be evacuated before the enemy. But the trains loaded with Jews do not come from districts already occupied by the foe. How else can a plain man construe this fact than that the Jews are spies, dangerous people, in short, our internal enemy? And so this one-year-old baby whose puffed-up, tiny hand hangs down from its mother's shoulder is also an enemy, just as is this sad girl wearily skulking in a corner, and this old man with his shaking head and wrinkled hands,—all these are our enemies, otherwise why should they have been deported before the arrival of the foe? Why such a peculiar selection of the passengers of the dreadful trains? I go from one porter to another, asking them who was brought on. The answer is the same: "Jews, spies...." The very arrival of such a train engenders an ill feeling toward the entire Jewish nation,—and how many such trains have arrived here lately! And if you were to stop and ask who established the guilt of these people, and whether it is thinkable that all these tens of thousands of men, women, and children should have been caught red-handed, no one will stop to listen to you. A Jew is a spy,—this is the only impression that becomes indelibly branded in the brains of the Russian population which witnesses the new tragedy of the Jewish nation. The effect of the passage of these trains is truly terrible, it is a series of systematic object-lessons of hatred....

When the crowd has quenched its hunger and thirst, a new problem presents itself: how to transport all this mass to the town and give them shelter. For this purpose a number of carriages are kept in readiness. The coachmen, all of them Jews, load the miserable luggage and try to accommodate the old, the sick, and the children. Now and then a bearded, husky driver would wipe away a tear; to one side, Jewish women weep frankly. The sorrowful procession sets out for the town. There the refugees will once more have to meet the Russians and endure questionings, insulting remarks and slaps in the face.... Will the Jewish nation stand all this? Yes, it will undoubtedly stand this frightful trial.

There is something in its inner nature that enables it to hold out under the most terrible conditions.

At the house of a representative of the Jewish community, I find several people who handle the transportation and distribution of the deported Jews.

"How many people have passed through your hands?"

"Several thousand. We get word by telegraph from the centres of deportation as to how many people we should keep and how many send further."

"Where do you get the means necessary for these operations?"

"The entire Jewish population of our town has imposed upon itself a systematic refugee tax. This source furnishes us 3,000 rubles monthly. Of course this is very little, ours is a poor town. Then we get financial aid from the Jewish communities, which do not have to help the deported directly. We have received several thousand rubles from Smolensk, Petrograd, Moscow, and elsewhere."

"And how about the Russian population, does it render you any assistance?"

"No, its attitude toward the deported is at best indifferent, and at worst hostile."

"And the Jews, do they not protest against this new tax?"

"Oh, no, not in the least. You have no idea to what an extent the feeling of solidarity grows among us in such cases. Here is an instance. A train with the deported arrived here yesterday. It was Saturday. That is, as you know, a sacred day for the Jews. Nevertheless, all our Jewish coachmen came to the station to take the newcomers to the town. We have asked them to come

122

to-day to get paid for their services. Not one of them appeared. And so it has been all along. There is not a Jewish coachman in the town who would take money in such a case. On the contrary, they would be insulted if they were not asked to do their bit. When the first train arrived, the present self-taxation was not yet in existence. We received the telegram suddenly. Nothing was in readiness. Our young people got busy and started canvassing the Jewish houses. And at once people brought all they could: tea, sugar, eggs, milk. We met the hungry ones with full hands. No, we cannot complain against the Jews; they do all they can, even the poorest."

The representative shows me a heap of telegrams. Their contents are brief: "To Rabbi so-and-so. Meet 900; meet 1000; meet 1100." Only the numbers differ....

"And where do you house those who remain here?"

"Well, we accommodate them in the Jewish school, in private homes, in rooms hired for the purpose. But here we met with a new obstacle. Our town is situated on the left bank of the river Dnyepr. Now a new order was issued to the effect that the deported should settle exclusively on the left bank. We had trouble enough, I warrant you. Fortunately, the local authorities have shown us some consideration and postponed the second deportation.... But to entrain worn-out people and send them anew into the unknown,—it is painful even to imagine it. Think of it: to grow accustomed to the place, to the people who take care of you,—and then again a train, a flashing of a station, and the final outrage of the arrival. Many say: 'Better to die than to resume our road again.' But we are forced to send them further, although nowadays it is hard to place the deported; all the towns are crowded, the congestion leads to diseases. Here, too, we have had several deaths...."

"Tell me," I said finally, "but you know, at least approximately, why these people are deported? It is impossible that this should be done for no earthly reason, simply because they happen to be Jews...."

How great was my repentance that I put this naïve question! I shall never, never forget the eyes which turned on me. There was in them a burning pain and another question: "Yes, for what crime? If we only knew it.... Perhaps, you will tell us? You are a Russian, you are in a better position to know...."

I got up quickly, shook hands, and left in silence, with a feeling of repulsion for myself and shame for my helplessness....

The Homeless Ones

By S. Yelpatyevsky

Sergey Yakovlevich Yelpatyevsky is a popular writer of realistic, and humanitarian tales and sketches. In his youth he was exiled to Siberia, and in 1910 he was imprisoned. He was born in 1854.

I

A party of Jews was brought to the province of Tavrida. Officially they are called "the deported"; the newspapers refer to them as "the homeless ones." At first came three thousand Jews from the province of Kovno. They were followed by Kurland Jews, and now about seven thousand Jews have been settled in the government of Tavrida. Other parties are expected....

They had wandered a long time before they reached their new place of residence. Obviously, the authorities who handled the deportation thought only of how to get rid of the Jews, and those on whom the newcomers were thrust had not been informed in time and did not know how to arrange to take care of them.

The first party, three thousand strong, stayed a while at Melitopol, then they were transported to Simferopol where they remained five days, and were finally distributed over the towns and townlets of northern Crimea.

It is told that one of the parties was assigned to Ekaterinoslav, but the authorities refused to accept the people and ordered them to proceed further. The local papers report that a group of deported Jews was transported from Pavlograd to Jankoy, then, according to an instruction from the Ministry of the Interior they were shipped to Voronezh....

There are many old men and women, many girls and mothers, and a large number of children in the party which has been brought here. All of them are miserable and exhausted, a number are ill, either because they had been sick when the catastrophe overtook them or because they fell ill on the way, and there are many pregnant women among them. As a result of their long wanderings, wives have lost their husbands and mothers their children and they eagerly question everybody about those dear to them.

Little has been written in the newspapers about the Jews deported from the zone of military activities, and so far little has been heard of either the state or the social organisations coming to the assistance of these "war sufferers," who feel the burden of war even more heavily than those who fled from the war-stricken districts on their own account. There was a vague statement that the Pirogov Society is aiding the Jews deported to the Government of Poltava and that meagre sums were contributed by the Union of Towns and the Ministry of the Interior,—that is all the newspapers have so far reported.

The burden of taking care of the newcomers fell entirely on the local Jewish communities. It was a heavy burden, for there are no more than about twenty thousand Jewish families in the entire government of Tavrida. These twenty thousand families had to take care and to support seven thousand homeless people, mostly small tradesmen and peddlers who had no time to liquidate their businesses and who could not take along any property, for bedding was the only thing they were allowed to carry.

They had to find housing facilities in all haste, to organise transportation and medical aid, and to solve the food and employment problems. An attempt was made to utilise the deported in agriculture, in which labour is nowadays exceedingly scarce in Crimea. But the old people and the children are not fit for agricultural work and it would take too long to train the able-bodied women. On the other hand, the largest and more prosperous Crimean towns, such as Simferopol and Sebastopol, Yalta, Yevpatoria, and Theodosia, where the deported Jews could easily find employment, are closed to the newcomers. Only the smaller and poorer towns and townlets where even the local Jews can scarcely get employment, are put at the disposal of the newcomers as their places of residence. There was even a project to settle a portion of these people in the city of Perekop. This town counts only one Jewish family among its population. It consists of a prison and several deserted shanties, and reminds one of that legendary Siberian town, which was made up of a single pillar erected as an indication of the site where the city was supposed to stand.

The local Jewish communities spend about fifty thousand rubles monthly on feeding the deported. This sum does not include the expenses of transpor-

127

tation and housing. The local communities applied to the Petrograd Committee, but it took upon itself only fifteen thousand rubles. The remaining thirty-five thousand are contributed by the Jews, who have also to support their specific cultural institutions as well as municipal institutions of a general character.

The representatives of the Simferopol Jewish community applied to the Governor of Tavrida for financial help. I do not know whether they were successful. Meanwhile, other parties of deported Jews are expected here, and how the Jews will be able to handle them, is more than I can tell.

The War has ruined many homes and made many men, women, and children homeless. But it would hardly be an exaggeration to say that fate has been most ruthless to these deported Jews. The so-called "refugees," after all, acted freely; they brought with them, if not what they wanted at least what they had time, what they were able to take; they could go wherever there was work. The refugees were everywhere welcomed and helped by both the authorities and the public organisations. Special days for the soliciting of donations were appointed and large sums collected. Wherever they went people tried to alleviate their sufferings. But the deportation of the Jews took place as if on the sly, without attracting any one's attention, without engaging the sympathies of the people at large to the degree which might be expected.

The deported proved a heavy burden not only for the Jewish but also for the Gentile population of the humble villages of the government of Tavrida, which were flooded by the newcomers. The prices of food, and the rent soared up, and competition among tradesmen and

128

small merchants grew more ruthless,—in a word, life here became much harder than the War alone would have made it.

II

As one observes these throngs of old men, children and pregnant women who are deported and tossed from one end of the country to the other, simply because they are Jews, one wonders to whom it brings profit or happiness. It is clear that it does no one any good and no one finds this wholesale deportation either just or necessary.

"In discussing the deportation of Jews the Minister of the Interior pointed out that this measure was not justified by the actual behaviour of the Jewish population, which is in general loyal to the country and cannot bear responsibility for the actions of criminal individuals, of whom unfortunately no nationality is free" (Yuzhnyia Vyedomosti, No 10). The same communication contains the following statements: "It was asserted that the wholesale accusation of the Jews as traitors is wholly groundless.... In view of this the council of Ministers, by an overwhelming majority, decided to make intercession to put an end to the deportation of the Jews."

Whether the Council of Ministers has interceded and whether its efforts were crowned with success,—I know not. The papers published several orders whereby separate groups of deported Jews were permitted to return to their former places of residence,—for instance, the deported Galician Jews were allowed to return to

Galicia,—but there was no general rescript which would put an end to the deportation....

The wholesale deportation of the Jews caused a great perplexity among the population of Crimea. Even people who are not over-sensitive to problems of truth and justice and whose sympathies are far from being broad, show signs of being stirred up. Suppose the Council of Ministers is mistaken, they say, and the presence of the Jews in the governments of Kovno and Kurland is really a danger for the State, but then do not Germans live in those provinces, in even larger numbers than Jews? Time and again we read in the newspapers of the friendly reception of the German armies by the German population of Kurland. There were also registered cases where penalties were imposed on individual persons who either showed too great an enthusiasm for the German troops or rendered them material services. Nevertheless, nothing was heard about the German population of the Government of Kurland being deported in a wholesale manner,—at least, not a single train with Kurland Germans has reached Crimea.

On the other hand,—so thinking people keep on arguing,—if the Jews have proved to be more German than the Germans themselves, and the Teutonic population of Kurland act like loyal Russian subjects, why then liquidate the land owned by the Crimean Germans, who have been living in Crimea for more than a century, who have never shown any disloyalty to Russia, who, furthermore, are separated from the German frontier by thousands of versts and who are, therefore, by no means able to inform the Germans from Germany about the movement of our troops in the provinces of Kurland and Kovno.

And once more rises the question: "In whose interests is all this done?"

The matter has also another aspect. How many Jews were deported—tens or hundreds of thousands—no one knows exactly; but seeing the large masses which are being shifted from place to place, people wonder how many cars were necessary to transport all these throngs. And then it occurs to them that all these trains could bring in enormous cargoes of coal, sugar, kerosene and other wares which are so badly needed here, and carry away grain and fruit, which are needed elsewhere, thus making life more liveable in many corners of our vast country.

And people who have the enviable capacity of not losing their equanimity under any circumstances, remark that in this fashion the Jewish problem is being settled and the Pale of Settlement removed.

"Here already the provinces of Voronezh and Penza are opened to Jews.... Little by little all of Russia will be opened up...."

Russian Jew, New York, 1910.
George Grantham Bain Collection.
Library of Congress, Washington, D.C. 20540 USA

The Jew

By M. Artzibashef

Mikhail Petrovich Artzibashef, the author of Sanine
was born in the year 1878 in Southern Russia. He is
widely read both in his own country and outside of
its borders. In 1905 he took part in the revolutionary movement, and was indicted, but escaped punishment because of the temporary success of the
popular movement at the end of that year.

I t so happened that the second platoon of the third
squad of the Ashkadar regiment found itself completely cut off from the main body of the army, and
this without the loss of a single cartridge or soldier.
How this came about, and why a group of men, fifteen
or twenty strong, had suddenly become an independent
fighting unit, none of them could tell.

At the outset, the entire Ashkadar regiment zealously
trudged throughout the long autumn night along an
interminable road, leading no one knew where, into
the dark, damp, and hostile distance. To smoke or to
converse was forbidden. In the dark, the black mass
of the regiment, bristling with its bayonets like some
huge, porcupine-like creature, crawled steadily onward,
filling the air with the shuffling of innumerable feet.
The men kept stumbling over each other, and swore
viciously in half tones; they slipped in the mud and

sank knee-deep into the wheel-tracks filled with cold water. "Some road!" they sighed quietly.

At dawn the regiment was brought to a halt and was stretched along the edge of a wide potato field, which the soldiers had never seen before. It was drizzling with sickening persistence, and the dark-blue distances, mildly sloping and mournful, were blurred in the haze of the rain. On both sides, as far as eye could reach, ranks of grey officers and soldiers were wretchedly soaking in the rain. Water was dripping from their sullen faces and it looked as though they were all weeping over their fate—the fate which had cast them upon this strange, unknown, God-forsaken field. In a few hours many of them will perhaps be lying dead amidst the half-rotted potato stems on the wet soil with their pallid faces upturned to the cold heavens, the very ones which now weep also over their dear, distant country.

Behind, a battery crew was vainly attempting to set the cannon which were sinking into the soaked ploughland. One could hear the hoarse angry voices, the cracking of whips, and the heavy, strained snorting of horses. In front of them lone officers wandered in drenched cloaks in the rain; still farther behind the curtain of rain and the thick fog there rumbled cannons and it was impossible to tell whether they belonged to the enemy or not. At times the shooting seemed to come from afar-off on the right. Then the rumble of the guns was deep and muffled like the sound of heavy iron balls rolling over the ground; at other times, the discharges were quite near and rent the air with a crash, bursting over the men's very heads, as it were.

The commander of the squad stood right in front of his men and kept lighting cigarettes shielding them with the skirts of his cloak. He did it so often that it seemed as if he had been vainly attempting to light the same cigarette for the last three hours. The soldiers were attentively looking at his back and were all morbidly anxious to help him. It was cold and damp, and they felt an incessant, nauseating gnawing in the pit of the stomach. It was not fear but an indefinite anguish, a sort of the-sooner-over-the-better feeling.

Several hours passed in this manner, but towards noon it all changed abruptly. Though the sky was still as grey as before and it drizzled continuously, it grew lighter, the clouds in one spot became white and shining and one felt that the sun was somewhere behind them. But amidst this cold white light a disquieting feeling pervaded the atmosphere and the gnawing anxiety was turning into unbearable agony. Suddenly, an aide-de-camp dashed past on a horse, covered with froth and fuzzy with dampness. Officers began to scurry back and forth; sharp commands were heard; and the bugles resounded.

"Well, comrades!" ... said some one in the ranks in a high, false tone of voice. Every one heard this exclamation and understood it, but no one turned around to see where it came from. The grey mass of people suddenly stirred, gave a sigh, surged like the sea whipped by a gale, and, sinking at each step into the mud, the entire regiment rolled forward, over the expanse of the shoreless fields which now suddenly looked strange and dreadful. The soldiers, their faces haggard and queer, were crossing themselves as they ran. They marched in disorder, and when they were stopped on the hillcrest, they turned the regiment into a confused mob of breathless and perplexed men. Some even forgot to lower their rifles.

Before them the hazy network of rain was still hanging and the distances stretched, strange and hostile. But now the fields were astir with flickering pale flames and a ceaseless scattered cracking of guns. In the grey sky a small black dot was discernible, seemingly motionless, but changing in size. When it grew larger, a faint buzzing was heard from above and made the soldiers turn their grey, ghastly faces upward.... Then a mighty buzzing suddenly resounded behind the regiment, and a Russian aeroplane flew over the heads of the men like a drenched bird. As the aeroplane rose higher and higher, the soldiers watched the distance between it and the small black dot far up in the sky grow smaller and smaller.

Voices were now heard from the ranks and when the black dot was rapidly beginning to grow smaller, sinking, as it were, in the sky and approaching the horizon, those voices became loud and gay.

"He don't like it, what! See him run for his life! Well done! Fine fellows!" ... was heard along the ranks.

The soldiers suddenly became lively and for a moment forgot about themselves and the uncertain fate that was in store for them.

"Why not put you on that aeroplane, Yermilich!... You'd be quite handy at it, wouldn't you!" the soldiers were poking fun at each other.

All at once a confused many-voiced cry and a disorderly crackling of rifles was heard ahead of them; then a crowd of soldiers came running from that direction, at first singly, then in groups, and finally in a mass. They belonged to another regiment of the same division. One could discern from afar their wide-open eyes, rounded mouths, and an expression of frantic terror on their pale faces.

The officers of the Ashkadar regiment, waving their swords and yelling something indistinct, were running over the washed-out field to meet the running men, but the grey crowd momentarily knocked them down, trampled upon them, completely covered them, and mingled itself with the Ashkadar men. And everything that, but a while ago, was so clear and important now became confused and meaningless.

Like the waters that wash off a dam pierced in but a single point, even so did the running soldiers confuse and sweep away the regiment. The Ashkadar men themselves were partly infected by the panic and began to run they knew not why, apparently possessed by that mysterious power which is transmitted from man to man and which pushes one from behind and compels him to run farther and farther, aimlessly and blindly.

The entire mass of men started down the slope, but having encountered the battery with a crew yelling and waving their hands, it swerved aside. Then as this mass ran into the regular line of soldiers, who were rapidly coming to meet them, their rifles carried at charge, it threw itself to one side, then to the other, then backwards and forwards and finally scattered over the fields, filling the air with mad outcries and disorderly shooting. It was at that very time that the second platoon of the third squad strayed from its regiment and its officers. Seventeen in all, instinctively keeping together, they found themselves outside of the battle-field in a narrow loamy ravine overgrown with dwarfish trees. The ravine was deep and had washed-out clay slopes.

High above it stretched a muddy, uneven strip of grey sky, which poured an unceasing rain upon the soaked red clay, upon the small wet birch trees, and the group of soldiers, who had lost their way and driven by inertia were hurrying further downward.

The soldiers, all reservists, were thick-set, bearded and pock-marked peasants from the governments of Kostroma and Novgorod and among them, was a dark little Jew, Hershel Mak, who alone thought and planned for the rest of them. All these country people taken right from the plough were unable to grasp how it all happened, and were not even sure whether anything had happened at all. They could not tell whether there was a battle or not, whether it was good or bad to be left without officers in this confounded ravine, and what would come of it all. Only Hershel Mak understood that there was a battle, that the front ranks came right under the crossfire of the machine-guns, that a panic resulted and that the Ashkadar regiment was knocked off its feet by a crowd of runaways. He knew that the regiment was broken up without a shot and that now they were left to their own fate, in a place which might well be within the very centre of the enemy's position. Hershel Mak was well aware of the fact that for the present no one would or could worry about them and that they must alone disentangle themselves from this mess,—and his versatile mind began at once to work to the utmost of its ability.

The rain was rushing in murmuring streams down the slopes of the ravine and along its bottom, and the noise of the water drowned the crackling of the machine-guns and the thundering of the cannon. The ravine extended further down, and apparently into the

138

forest, for the trees were becoming thicker, and on the ground a deep layer of half-decayed leaves was mingled with the clay. Once or twice, a heavy buzzing was heard overhead, and the soldiers involuntarily lifted their eyes, but there was no aeroplane in sight, and one could not tell whether it was the enemy or not.

Hershel Mak was walking behind the others, and was deep in thought.

"What are we going to do when we meet the enemy? When we were with the regiment, we knew what to do.... But we don't know the high military rules! Maybe, we shouldn't fight at all,—maybe, according to the high military rules it is necessary to retreat a bit?... How is one to tell I'd like to know."

Just then on the opposite bank of the stream which in its overflowing formed shallow muddy puddles something dark began to flicker among the trees, and the enemy soldiers in light grey cloaks, and varnished helmets protected with linen covers came forward. This was an enemy detachment which had also strayed away from its regiment. A non-commissioned officer, husky and red-bearded, was in charge of it. The Germans' gait was also uncertain. They walked with rifles carried at charge, timidly looking about and were just going to stop to talk over their situation, when they noticed the reddish-grey cloaks and the bayonets.

"Halt!" yelled out a flaxen-haired Kostroma peasant. He did it so forcefully that two crows flew off in fright and rose high above the ravine.

Hershel Mak nearly fell into the water. The red and the grey soldiers separated by about fifty steps and a small, turbid, rain-beaten rivulet were eyeing each other with amazement rather than with terror. Thin scattered cries of terror and dismay were heard from the other side, and all at once it grew still with an ominous strained stillness.

"Listen ... eh," ... whispered Hershel Mak, touching the gun of the Kostroma reservist. But at this very moment, the soldiers as if in response to a command stepped back a pace or two, got down on their knees and an uneven crackling of guns rent the damp air.

The flaxen-haired Kostroma peasant and another soldier, a father of a large family, nick-named "uncle," threw up their arms and fell heavily upon the soaked clay.

The first was killed on the spot, but as to the "uncle," he clutched his abdomen, sat up and began to howl in a thin, piercing voice: "Bro-o-thers!"

And the soldiers were seized with a savage anger, immense and terrible, similar to the nervous fury with which one tramples upon a snake. Scattered bullets began flying amidst the wet trees, and wild outcries filled the air. The bullets hissed far over the forest and sank with a swish into the clay; birch leaves, quietly circling, were falling to the ground where three light-grey figures were writhing in convulsions of pain and horror.

The husky non-commissioned officer was the first among these to cease stirring. He lay there with his face stuck in the cold mud of the stream. A volley of bullets, still more uneven than the first answered it, and presently single shots, interrupted by furious outcries of pain, by groans of the wounded and rattling of the dying came from both sides.

Pale flames flickered everywhere; the bark was being ripped from the small birch trees; here and there were seen ghastly distorted faces and shivering hands hurriedly fussing with the guns. The biting odour of blood and gun-powder filled the air, and a bluish smoke rose slowly to the sky, passing through the twigs shivering, as it were, with fear, and under the birches there lay two groups of men, charging their guns, shooting, slaying one another, and strewing the wet earth with crippled, writhing, moaning bodies.

Suddenly the shooting ceased just as unexpectedly as it had begun. There was no one upon the clearing except the wounded, and the dead. The reddish soldiers hid behind the stones and the grey behind the trees.

The fire ceased. The hearts of the men beat rapidly and painfully with a vicious inhuman terror, but no one fired a single shot. An hour passed and then another. The men lay silently behind the stones and the trees, each group eyeing the enemy sharply and closely watching their slightest movements.

"Uncle" alone, his back leaning on a trunk of a tree, was moaning plaintively and softly like a fly caught in a spider's web. And on the other side a young soldier was making severe attempts to lift up his body out of the mud puddle, while the eyes of his pale youthful face were already covered with the film of death. But no one paid the slightest attention to either of them. Each one felt upon himself the keen, merciless eye of the enemy and dared not budge or even stretch out a benumbed foot. A grey soldier attempted once to change his place, whereupon three shots thundered from the other side, and the man only turned over and remained still. Later two men were killed, one on each side, and again everything grew still.

The clatter of the rain alone was heard, as though, invisible to the eye, some one wept bitterly in the forest. The hours were passing, and the nervous tension grew intolerable, assuming the intensity of agony. It was quite apparent that things could not go on in this way much longer, and every one knew that whoever would lift his head would be killed on the spot. Lord only knows the odd and horrible thoughts that were passing in these terror-stricken, muddled minds.

Hershel Mak felt very keenly that he was eager to live; that like the rest of these men, he had a father and mother and also his own little desires, remote from this place and sacred to him alone. He was also sorry for "uncle" and for that dying German, who lay in the puddle, and who had been killed, perhaps by a bullet from "uncle's" rifle.

The hours were passing and the unbearable nervous horror grew, and the inner tension, terrible and so taut that it seemed to be ready to snap every second, was beginning to turn into a sort of nightmare, which makes one shiver all over, which dims one's eyes with red mist, which banishes all fear of death and suffering and turns all that is human into an elemental, savage fury.

At the very moment, when the tension reached its highest point and the nightmare was about to pass in a ruthless engagement, Hershel Mak, unable to control his strained nerves any longer began to pray plaintively in the tongue of his forefathers. "Shma Isroel! Shma Isroel!" ... His comrades did not understand him and glanced at him in terror, as at a madman, but from the

142

opposite side another frightened and plaintive voice answered him in Jewish: "A Jew!... A Jew!..."

Hershel Mak's heart fell within him. The mad joy that took hold of him is indescribable. It was undefiled human joy that filled him to the brim, when from the place whence he expected only death and hatred there came familiar human words. Forgetting the deathly peril, he sprang to his knees, threw up his arms and cried out, as if responding to a voice heard in the desert.

"I!... I!..."

A shot crashed; but it was only Mak's cap, that jumped up and landed in the mud puddle. From beyond the stream and the trees a typical head with ears projecting from under the varnished helmet looked straight at him.

"Don't shoot!... Don't shoot!" yelled Hershel Mak in Russian, German and Jewish all at once, waving his hands frantically. And the other Jew, in a long light-grey cloak was also yelling something to his fellow-soldiers. Now not one but about ten pairs of eyes looked at Hershel Mak, with astonishment and sudden joy. A vague, faint hope was seen in these frightened human eyes, which suddenly became simple and sympathetic. Then Hershel Mak and the Jew in the light-grey cloak rushed to the clearing and, splashing in the water, trustingly ran to each other. They met between the two ranks of still hostile gun-barrels and embraced each other in a fit of unreasoning human gladness. "Are you a Jew?" asked the grey soldier. They kept looking at each other like two old friends who met where they least expected to find each other.

In the twilight, after the soldiers gathered up their dead and wounded, they went each their own way along the ravine, now blue with the evening fog. Those in the rear kept looking back at the enemy, suspiciously eyeing them, and nervously clutching with their hands the cold muzzles of their guns.

Only Hershel Mak and the Jew in the light-grey cloak walked calmly. Hershel chattered like a monkey, joining now one now another of the soldiers. He was saying something about his joy, about the great mission of Judaism. But no one listened to him, and one of the soldiers said good-naturedly: "Go to the devil, you dirty Jew."

www.ingramcontent.com/pod-product-compliance
Lightning Source LLC
Chambersburg PA
CBHW071956170626
46813CB00005B/1899

* 9 7 8 0 9 5 6 4 0 1 0 2 1 *